To appoint unto them that mourn in Zion, to give unto them beauty for ashes, the oil of joy for mourning, the garment of praise for the spirit of heaviness; that they might be called trees of righteousness, the planting of the LORD, that he might be glorified.

—Isaiah 61:3 (KJV)

NOW YOU'RE IN MY ARMS

LESLIE GOULD

NOW
YOU'RE IN
MY ARMS

DUMONT-OLSON-CONNOR-JOHNSTON
Family Tree

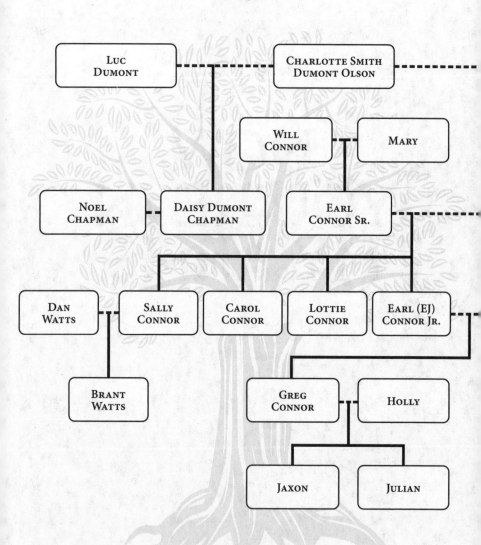

LUC DUMONT

CHARLOTTE SMITH DUMONT OLSON

WILL CONNOR

MARY

NOEL CHAPMAN

DAISY DUMONT CHAPMAN

EARL CONNOR SR.

DAN WATTS

SALLY CONNOR

CAROL CONNOR

LOTTIE CONNOR

EARL (EJ) CONNOR JR.

BRANT WATTS

GREG CONNOR

HOLLY

JAXON

JULIAN

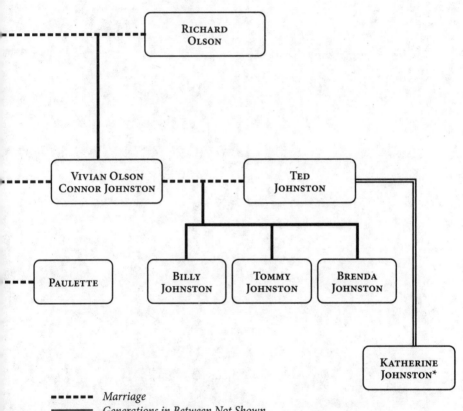

RICHARD OLSON

VIVIAN OLSON CONNOR JOHNSTON

TED JOHNSTON

PAULETTE

BILLY JOHNSTON

TOMMY JOHNSTON

BRENDA JOHNSTON

KATHERINE JOHNSTON*

------- Marriage
======= Generations in Between Not Shown

1906: Charlotte Smith marries Luc Dumont
1914: Luc Dumont dies
1916: Charlotte Smith Dumont marries Richard Olson
1936: Earl Connor Sr. marries Vivian Olson
1943: Earl Connor Sr. dies
1947: Ted Johnston marries Vivian Olson Connor

*Katherine Johnston is Ted Johnston's great-niece

CHAPTER ONE

appy February!" Debbie Albright called out as she opened the back door of the Whistle Stop Café. She stomped her boots and then stepped over the threshold. "Can you believe this snow? It's close to a half foot already." She pulled the door closed against the storm.

Janet Shaw, Debbie's best friend, stepped out of the kitchen, wearing a white apron adorned with red and pink hearts. She held up an identical apron for Debbie and grinned. "Happy February to you too!"

Debbie had always loved February. January was over. Valentine's Day was only two weeks away, which meant decorating sugar cookies and making homemade valentines. This year, for the second year in a row, plans for the Valentine's Day Dance were in full swing.

And for the first Valentine's Day in twenty-two years, she had a sweetheart. Yes, her romance with Greg Connor just kept getting better and better.

February was going to be an amazing month.

A half hour later, Debbie flipped the Open sign. An hour after that, she and Janet sat at the counter. "I didn't expect it to be this slow," Janet said.

"Business might still pick up." Debbie wrapped her hands around her hot mug of coffee. "If not, we knew there would be days like this. And it's certainly not the first time. Remember last month's storm?" Buying the café together had been a risk for the two lifelong friends—one that had paid off overall.

Janet glanced out the window at the large, falling snowflakes and then back at Debbie. "Let's talk about the dance. How about if we host an event next Saturday to make decorations for the lobby? I have a box of doilies and old valentines we can use. We'll decorate the depot lobby for the entire month with what people make."

"Sounds lovely." Debbie took a sip of coffee.

"I was going through photographs of last year's dance that Kim gave me from the museum collection and thought it would be fun to make a display," Janet said. "I'll print the photos in black and white and use black paper and photo corners to make it look like a 1940s scrapbook. Then I can mount them on a trifold board."

"Perfect!" Debbie loved how creative Janet was, and not just with her baking.

The bell on the café's front door dinged. A couple Debbie didn't recognize stepped inside.

Debbie slid off her stool and reached for two menus. "Welcome!" she said as she started toward them.

The next customer through the door was Harry Franklin with his dog, Crosby, trailing behind. "Harry, what are you doing out in this snow?" Debbie gently chided, then grabbed a mug and the coffeepot. He was a young ninety-seven years, but he still shouldn't be risking a fall.

"You can't keep me away from a hearty breakfast and a good cup of coffee." He grinned.

"Is Patricia joining you?" Patricia Franklin was his doting granddaughter.

"Not this morning." He sat at his usual table. "Her car's in the shop."

"How was the walk over?" Debbie asked.

"Just fine. People are shoveling their sidewalks. The snow is fluffy—not icy. I didn't have a problem." He reached down to pet the dog. "Neither did Crosby."

Paulette, Greg's widowed mother who was also a server at the café, came in at nine and joined Debbie and Janet in the kitchen. Greg's father, EJ, had died years ago.

"Goodness," Paulette said. "What a morning." She took off her coat. "I stopped by my storage unit to retrieve the rest of the boxes full of stuff Jaxon helped me go through. There are a couple that belonged to my mother-in-law I want to give to Greg. EJ ended up with a lot of Vivian's things. I was going to give everything to his sister Sally, but when her husband died she downsized to an apartment at Good Shepherd." Paulette took a deep breath. It wasn't like her to talk so quickly. "Anyway, when I arrived at Greg's, I realized I'd forgotten my key. He's at the basketball tournament with Jaxon, and Julian spent the night at a friend's house. I had to trudge around to the back porch and leave the boxes there, in the enclosed part." Her eyes twinkled. "I don't know what I was thinking, clearing out the rest of my storage unit on a day like today.'"

Debbie gave her a sympathetic look. She would have been happy to help.

As Paulette hung up her coat, Janet said, "There's a new apron for you on your hook."

Debbie put her arm around Janet. "It matches ours."

"How fun." Paulette grabbed her new apron, pulled it over her dark hair, and struck a pose, followed by a grin.

Business gradually picked up and held steady until just before two—an hour before closing—when the last customer left. Janet left soon after, and then Debbie shooed Paulette, who needed to get her giveaway boxes to the thrift store, out the door. Then she texted Greg.

How's the tournament going?

He texted back, Great! The last game just ended. We won. See you at swing dance class. They'd signed up for a refresher course to be ready for the Valentine's Day event.

Debbie "loved" his text and slipped her phone into her pocket. There was no one in the world she'd rather dance with than Greg.

As Debbie flipped the sign to Closed, Kim Smith, curator of the Dennison Depot Museum, stepped through the front door and asked, "Do you have a minute?"

"Sure." Debbie straightened the sign. "What's up?"

"I'm working on an exhibit about women on the home front and wanted to feature a war widow from the area. I thought of Greg's grandmother. Paulette said one time that her mother-in-law belonged to the church knitting circle and made socks, gloves, and scarves—that sort of thing—for the soldiers. I'd love to feature her. Do you think Greg or Paulette have photographs and a couple of artifacts we could use?"

"Paulette just dropped off a couple boxes of Vivian's things at Greg's today, so maybe."

"Would you mind asking him?" Kim's voice wavered. "And perhaps help me with that part of the exhibit?"

Debbie tilted her head. "Is everything okay?"

"I think so. Barry hasn't been feeling well and had a round of tests yesterday. Just now, I realized I'm more stressed than I thought."

Debbie reached for her friend's hand. "Of course I'll help."

"Thank you."

"I know how much you're looking forward to the dance on Valentine's Day," Debbie said. "I hope the doctor can sort out Barry's medical concerns by then."

"So do I." Kim's eyes grew teary. "He's been having an irregular heartbeat." She blinked the tears away. "Dancing might be out, and I don't want to dance without him."

Debbie gave Kim a hug and then said, "Greg and I signed up for the refresher class at the community center. It starts this afternoon. I'll ask him about you featuring his grandmother in the exhibit and let you know."

After Kim headed back to the museum, Debbie got to work cleaning the café and prepping for Monday morning. Then she headed home. The snow had stopped falling and the sun had come out, creating a sparkly white landscape. As she made her way down the shoveled sidewalks, she breathed in the crisp air. By the time she reached her bungalow, she was a little chilled. After turning up the heat, she made herself a cup of tea and called her mother. Her parents lived just outside of town.

After saying hello, Debbie asked, "How are you and Dad doing with the snow?"

"Just fine, although I have a little bit of a cold. We're going to miss church tomorrow."

Debbie gave her mom a synopsis of her day. After the two caught up, she said, "Let me know if you need anything." They said their goodbyes, and Debbie ended the call.

She thought about Kim's request. There didn't seem to be a reason to wait to ask in person, so why not text Greg now about Kim wanting to include his grandmother as a war widow in her upcoming home-front exhibit and asking Debbie to help with it?

Debbie sent the text, opened the novel she'd started yesterday, and sipped her tea. Fifteen minutes later, Greg responded.

I'D BE HONORED IF KIM INCLUDED GRANDMA. IN FACT, I JUST DROPPED JAXON OFF AT THE HOUSE AND HE FOUND TWO BOXES MOM LEFT ON THE BACK PORCH. I'M OFF TO CHECK A WORK SITE. LET'S MEET AT THE COMMUNITY HALL. DON'T FORGET YOUR DANCING SHOES!

Debbie replied, I CAN'T WAIT TO FIND OUT MORE ABOUT YOUR GRANDMOTHER. AND TO PUT ON MY DANCING SHOES. She sent Kim a confirmation message and then went upstairs to change.

When she arrived at the community hall, Greg's pickup wasn't in the parking lot. She went on inside, sat in a chair along the perimeter of the hall, and changed out of her boots into her shoes. Then she took off her long coat. She wore an A-line, knee-length sapphire blue dress with a full skirt. It was one of a few she owned that worked for swing dancing. Spinning around with the skirt flared always made her feel like a girl again.

More dancers congregated, and one of the instructors started the music. She appeared to be in her late fifties. "Welcome!" The woman gestured. "Please gather around."

Debbie glanced toward the door. Where was Greg? She joined the other students in a half circle around the instructors.

The woman said, "I'm Meg Sinclair." She looked familiar. Debbie had definitely seen her around town. Meg wore a bright red dress, matching lipstick, and black pumps. She'd piled her blondish-gray hair on top of her head.

She motioned to the man next to her. "And this is my husband, Jeff."

He gave a wave. Jeff appeared to be a few years older than Meg, and he looked familiar too.

"We took up swing dancing thirty years ago," Meg said. "We taught classes here for years and recently decided to do it again."

The door opened and Greg stepped into the hall, giving Debbie a smile. Relieved, she waved. Then he sat down to change his shoes.

Meg explained more about the class, and just as she asked the men to form a line on the far end of the hall and the women on the opposite side, Greg was at Debbie's side. He gave her a half hug then followed the other men.

Jeff and Meg demonstrated the rock step, a basic move where the dancer steps forward with one foot then steps back with the other. Jeff then stood with his back to the men, and Meg stood facing him, leading the students in practice. Next they worked on triple steps to the left and triple steps to the right.

Debbie kept her eyes on Greg, who looked as handsome as ever in his black slacks and blue button-down shirt.

Meg switched the music to Glenn Miller's "In the Mood" and told everyone to find a partner. Greg took five quick steps to Debbie's side. She turned to face him. He placed a hand on her lower back, and she placed a hand on his shoulder. He clasped her free hand with his. They grinned at each other.

As Meg and Jeff stepped into position, Meg called out, "Rock step. Release your partner. Rock backward and outward for the two triple steps, extending your arm…"

"Aha." Debbie drew her arm in. "I remember where I saw Meg and Jeff before—at the Valentine's Dance a year ago."

Greg had a puzzled expression on his face.

"Do you remember them?"

He shook his head.

Debbie did. They definitely knew what they were doing then—and now.

Meg called out, "Triple step."

Greg stepped, and Debbie followed. Or tried to. She stepped on Greg's foot. He laughed and added an extra quick step.

Debbie cringed. "Sorry."

"That's okay," Greg said. "You can step on my foot anytime."

Meg called out, "Rock step."

Greg and Debbie glided through the next several moves, but then she stepped on Greg's foot again.

"Sorry," she repeated.

"Don't worry about it." Greg placed his hand on Debbie's back again. "I was off a beat."

After the class, Greg kept hold of Debbie's hand. "You did great. I'm a little rusty though."

"No," Debbie answered. "I'm the one who stepped on your feet."

Greg led her to the chairs. "Want to come by for a while? You could help me go through Grandma's boxes and see if there's anything Kim can use in the exhibit. The boys are making dinner."

"Sure," Debbie said. "I'd like that."

When they reached Greg's house, he took Debbie's arm and held tight as they walked up the icy steps. Greg opened the front door and Debbie stepped in first, inhaling a spicy aroma.

"I'm home," Greg called out. "Debbie's here too!"

Julian, who was in eighth grade, dashed out of the kitchen. "Hi, Dad! Hi, Debbie. The chili's ready." He tore past them and up the open staircase.

"Did Jaxon start the corn bread?" Greg called out after him.

"Noooo!" Julian's voice faded as he reached the landing.

After they hung up their coats, Greg called up the stairs, "Jaxon, would you start the corn bread, please?"

A moment later, Jaxon came thundering down the stairs. "Sorry. After I shoveled the snow, I got distracted by the Ohio State game. They're playing Indiana." He slid into the kitchen in his stocking feet.

"Thanks for doing it now," Greg called after him. He motioned to two cardboard boxes on the glass-top coffee table in the living room and said to Debbie, "We might as well go through these before dinner."

Debbie nodded and sat down on the sofa. Greg sat next to her and pulled a box closer. He took his key chain from his pocket, opened up his small Swiss Army knife, and cut the packing tape. Then he reached inside and pulled out a piece of paper. After a moment he smiled. "Mom made an inventory list. This box is all my grand-mother's diaries, from 1939 to 1985."

"No family treasures?" Debbie teased. "Although these are trea-sures in their own way."

Greg chuckled. "The fanciest thing Grandma owned was her wedding ring."

"From your Grandpa Earl or Grandpa Ted?" Earl had gone off to war, leaving Greg's grandmother with four children when he was killed in combat. Later, she had married Ted Johnston, who had served with Earl overseas and was the only father Greg's dad, EJ—Earl Junior—had ever known.

Greg furrowed his brow. "I'm guessing from Grandpa Ted." He lifted out a diary and opened it. "This is the first one." He turned the book toward Debbie. "She started it the day my aunt Sally, her first child, was born in 1938." He leafed through the pages. "The first entry is full of emotion, and then the next few are mostly about the weather and farmwork. Lots of facts."

"But few feelings?"

"Looks that way," he said.

"Not everyone can express their emotions, even in the pages of a private diary. Perhaps she was just more comfortable recording daily events."

"That makes sense. Especially when you consider she had four children and worked on a farm. I'm surprised she had time to do even this much." He returned the diary to the box.

"These will take a while to go through," Debbie said. "But I can narrow it down by focusing only on the dates during the war."

Greg reached for the second box, and one flap popped up as he gripped it. He opened the box and retrieved the inventory list. "Photographs and letters." He lifted out a stack of envelopes. "These are from Grandpa Earl." He pulled out another packet. "And these are Grandma's letters to him." Then he fished out a single envelope. "This is from Grandpa Ted, postmarked November 1946."

He searched in the box a moment more and came up with a third packet. "These are all from someone named Daisy Chapman." He slid the top envelope from the stack and opened it. "It's signed 'your sister, Daisy.'" He frowned. "I didn't know Grandma had a sister named Daisy—or any sister at all."

"How odd," Debbie said. "Maybe Daisy was just a friend, but they were close as sisters."

Greg looked thoughtful. "Maybe. It will take quite a bit of time to go through the letters." He set the last packet next to the other ones on the coffee table. "But let's look at the photographs now. We can put anything from the World War II era aside for you to show to Kim, same as the diaries, and get you two started on your project."

Debbie reached into the box and pulled out a stack of photos. For the next fifteen minutes they sorted through the pictures. They ranged from the mid-1930s to the late 1980s and weren't in any sort of chronological order. Fortunately, most had a date stamped on the bottom.

When the timer rang for the corn bread, Greg put down his stack of photographs and headed into the kitchen while Debbie reached into the box to see if there was anything else. Her hand bumped against something soft and round.

She stood and looked into the box. At the bottom was a ball of yarn still attached to a scarf that hadn't been finished. One needle was attached to the last row. She smiled. Just last month, she and Janet had solved a mystery involving a person who was completing people's unfinished projects and blessing random Dennison residents with her handiwork.

Perhaps this scarf was one Vivian had been making for a soldier for the war effort, if not for Earl himself. But wouldn't she have finished it?

Debbie checked Paulette's inventory. There was no mention of the scarf.

The yarn was thick and uneven and a grayish white. As she examined it more closely, she noticed odd sequences of stitches, a mix of bumps and vees in multiple rows. She knew little about knitting, but it didn't look right. The needle fell out of the ball of yarn, and Debbie thrust it back in—hitting something in the middle that wouldn't allow the needle to go through. She dug her finger around, but the ball was tightly wound and she didn't make much progress.

Greg stepped into the living room. "What's that?"

Debbie held up the ball. "There's something in the middle." She started unwinding it. After a few minutes and a big pile of loose yarn, a ring with an enormous stone fell into her lap.

She picked it up. "Does this look familiar?"

"No," Greg said. "I've never seen it before. But I don't imagine it's worth anything. My grandmother was a farmer's wife. She didn't have expensive jewelry."

The stone did seem dull. The metal was in good shape and not tarnished at all. Small stones stretched halfway around the band on each side. As the ring caught the light, the big stone shimmered a little. She glanced up at Greg. "You should get this appraised just in case it's not costume jewelry. But even costume jewelry can be valuable, if it's by certain designers."

He nodded. "I wonder where it came from. And why was it in the middle of a ball of yarn?"

CHAPTER TWO

"I have hot chocolate ready," Debbie said. "Or hot water for tea."

Greg had sent Vivian's boxes home with Debbie the night before, and they agreed he'd bring his mom by after church so Paulette could see the knitting project.

Paulette took off her snowy boots and set them on the mat by the door then changed into a pair of slippers she pulled from her tote bag. "Hot chocolate for me," she said.

"Same for me, please," Greg said. His mother handed him a pair of slippers as well, which he dutifully donned.

Debbie grinned, loving how comfortable and at-home Greg and Paulette had become in her house. She took their coats and then motioned toward the dining room. "The scarf is on the table along with the two boxes."

Greg led the way, and he and Paulette stopped at the table while Debbie continued on to the kitchen. When she returned with three mugs of hot chocolate on a tray, her guests were sitting down and Paulette was examining the scarf and ball of yarn, which Debbie had rewound and stuck the needle back into last evening. "I've never seen this before. I have no idea how it ended up with Vivian's things."

"Could it have been in the bottom of the box?" Greg asked. "Maybe you missed it."

Paulette shook her head. "I made the inventories as I placed things in the boxes. So I would have seen this. It looks as if it *could* have belonged to Vivian. But it wasn't in the box when I dropped it off." She glanced from Greg to Debbie.

Greg shrugged. "I can't explain it."

"How about if I call Sally and see if she knows anything?" Paulette asked.

"Good idea," Greg said.

Paulette stood and walked into the living room as she placed the call.

"Have you met Aunt Sally?" Greg asked. "Watts is her last name."

Debbie shook her head. "I know she's Vivian's oldest daughter."

"Yes," Greg said. "Her husband, my uncle, passed away about six months ago. They moved to Columbus for his medical treatments a long time ago. My cousin Brant, their son, lives there."

"I'm sorry about your uncle. Your mom said Sally is at Good Shepherd now."

"That's right," Greg answered.

Paulette stepped into the dining room and turned her attention to Greg. "Brant's here for the day. He's going to give Sally a ride over. She said she wanted to see the scarf and ball of yarn in person."

The two arrived fifteen minutes later. Sally had short gray hair, faded blue eyes, and a slight frame. Brant was shorter than Greg, but Debbie could have guessed they were cousins. They had the same dark hair and brilliant blue eyes.

After Greg made introductions, Debbie asked Brant if he could stay for a cup of hot chocolate.

"I'll stay," he said. "But I'll pass on the hot chocolate."

"Would you like some, Sally?"

"No, thank you." Her gaze landed on the ball of yarn and the scarf. She perked up. "I had a hunch EJ took these years ago." She stepped animatedly to the table and picked up the items.

This time Paulette gasped. "What are you suggesting, Sally? That he took something he shouldn't have from his—your—own mother?"

Sally shrugged, squeezed the ball of yarn, and took the needle out.

Greg crossed his arms. "Debbie and I found this knitting project in one of the boxes Mom left on my porch yesterday."

"It wasn't in the box when it was in my possession. Someone put it in the box after I put it on Greg's porch." Paulette stood up straighter. "EJ didn't take the ball of yarn or the ring inside it."

Sally's eyebrows rose. "So you know about the ring?"

Brant looked confused. "Ring? What does that have to do with a ball of yarn and an ugly scarf?"

Greg took a small white box out of his jacket pocket and opened it. "Is this what you're looking for?"

"Yes." Sally plunged the needle through the center of the ball of yarn and placed it back on the table. "Did you find the ring inside the yarn?"

"Debbie did." Greg took the ring from atop the cotton inside the box and passed it to Sally.

She snatched it out of his hand and held it up to the light. "Daddy acquired it somehow and gave it to Mama, sometime after they were married." She closed her fist around the ring. "It, along with the scarf and ball of yarn, went missing sometime around when Mama died. I have no idea if it was before or after."

Greg asked, "Where did Grandma keep the ring?"

Sally chuckled. "In the ball of yarn."

"All the time?"

"As far as I know," Sally answered. "I never saw it anywhere else. I asked her why she didn't keep it in her jewelry box, and she said it belonged in the ball of yarn. She never explained why." Sally turned to Paulette. "Maybe you just overlooked all this in EJ's things."

"I did not." Paulette had a determined expression on her face. "I've gone through EJ's possessions multiple times. Today is the first time I've seen either."

Sally clucked her tongue and sat down with the ring still in her hand. "I always thought EJ believed the ring should go to him since he was the only boy, and Mama named him after Daddy."

Paulette exhaled and then spoke slowly. "EJ never mentioned the ring to me. Not once." She held out her left hand. She wore a simple gold band on her ring finger. "This was Vivian's from Earl Sr. She gave it to EJ to give to me."

"Well, sure," Sally said. "I know that. I just thought he expected her to give him the big ring too. But she intended for me to have it."

"Did you ever hear EJ say he expected to inherit the ring?" Debbie asked, then wondered if she should have said anything. This seemed to be a family discussion. But it was happening in her home, wasn't it?

Sally squared her shoulders.

"Mom?" Brant asked. "Was it in the will or anything?"

"Not exactly." Sally stared straight ahead.

Paulette said, "Katherine Johnston stopped by my house Friday asking about family heirlooms that have disappeared." She turned to Debbie and said, "Katherine is Grandpa Ted's niece, the daughter of his older brother." She continued, "Katherine wouldn't say what she was looking for in particular, but perhaps she was looking for this ring. It seems pretty coincidental, doesn't it?"

Sally said, "She's been after me about Johnston family heirlooms too. But this ring was from Daddy to my mother. It has nothing to do with my stepdad or the Johnston family."

Greg sat down across from Sally. "I would love to hear, since we're all together, what you remember about the scarf and the ring."

"Me too," Brant added.

After a long pause, Sally put her free hand on the scarf. "According to Ted, my stepdad, he brought this scarf, attached to the ball of yarn with the ring inside, back from Europe after the war. Ted never knew how it all landed in my father's possession, but he believed it was sometime after they landed in North Africa but before Daddy was killed, of course. Ted also had the letters from Mama to Daddy that Daddy asked Ted to return to Mama, if anything happened to him. Ted gave everything to Mama the day he arrived on our farm."

Debbie had to think that sentence through. Earl had asked Ted to return Vivian's letters if anything happened to him. Ted had done that, along with the other items. Later, she knew, Ted and Vivian had married. Ted became stepdad to Greg's father, Aunt Sally, and two other children. Then Ted and Vivian had gone on to have three more children together.

"But Grandpa died in Tunisia." Greg leaned toward Sally. "Why would Ted carry a ball of yarn with a ring in the middle and an unfinished scarf through the rest of his North Africa campaign and then back to England and on through France and Germany? The letters I could understand."

Sally shrugged. "I don't know—I just know he did. Ted squeezed it all into his rucksack with the letters after Daddy died and hung on to everything for—" She counted the years on her fingers. "Daddy died in 1943, so through '44 and '45 and half of '46. He showed up on our farm in June of 1946." She looked up. "That's all I can say. Ted and Mama never talked about it much with us kids beyond that." Sally rubbed her hand across the scarf. "This all went missing, along with the ring, around the time Mama died—I'm not sure if it was before or after. The last time I checked, all were in her bottom drawer a couple of months before she passed."

She held up the ring in the palm of her hand. "It seems it was worth something but not a lot. I never knew how much. Its value is sentimental."

Greg leaned back in his chair. "I plan to talk to a jeweler about it tomorrow."

"That's a good idea." She squeezed her hand around the ring.

"I'll find out what the value is, and then we can talk," Greg said. "Does that sound all right?"

She nodded and opened her hand. "Mama did plan to give the ring to me, as the oldest."

"Mom." Brant's expression was firm as he met his mother's gaze. "Did Grandma really say that?"

Sally locked eyes with him. "Yes." She put the ring on the table and pulled out her phone. After she took a photo, she raised her head and glanced around the room.

Debbie motioned to the stacks of diaries and letters. "Sally. Paulette. Did either of you ever read through all of these?"

Paulette shook her head. "I didn't even realize EJ had them until after he passed away."

"I'd planned to read them, but then Dan was diagnosed with cancer for the first time right after Mama passed away, and I gave everything to EJ when we moved." Sally crossed her arms. "Lottie thought I went through Mama's diaries and letters and said there wasn't anything important in any of them, but I never told her that."

Lottie was one of Sally and EJ's sisters, Debbie recalled. She couldn't imagine not immediately going through a loved one's papers after they died, but perhaps, even aside from Sally's husband falling ill, it had all been too emotional right after Vivian died.

Brant stood and said to his mother, "I should start home. Do you want me to give you a ride back to Good Shepherd?"

"Please." Sally stood too.

"Could you drop me off at home?" Paulette asked.

"It's okay, Mom." Greg stood too. "I can give you a ride home."

"No," she said. "I'll get a ride with Brant."

Greg shook Brant's hand and gave Sally a hug. "We'll figure this out—and honor Grandma in the process."

Sally clasped his hand. "Thank you. That's what we need to keep in mind."

Debbie told both Sally and Brant how nice it was to meet them. Then she gave Paulette a hug and said, "I'll see you tomorrow."

As she shut the door behind them, she said to Greg, "Do you mind if I call Ian?" Ian was Dennison's police chief and Janet's husband.

Greg picked up the ring and positioned it back in the box. "The ring hasn't been stolen. It seems as though it's been returned."

"Right. But maybe Ian can advise us on what to focus on now. And how much he thinks the disappearance of the ring thirty years ago has to do with figuring out how it ended up on your porch."

Greg picked up his mug. "Sure. It can't hurt to brainstorm a little with a professional."

"I'll ask Janet to come over too, since no crime has been committed, so it doesn't matter if she's in on the conversation. She's not a professional, but she's bound to have some helpful ideas."

Janet, who wore a black beret tilted over her blond hair, led the way into the house, carrying a heart-shaped charcuterie board, followed by Ian.

Debbie rolled her eyes at Janet. "You had time to put that together before you headed over here?"

Janet batted her eyelashes. "It's incredible what I can do, right?"

"Don't believe her," Ian said, grinning. "We were supposed to go to her parents' house for dinner, but they aren't feeling well."

"Oh?"

"It's just a cold," Janet said. "But they didn't want to share, which I appreciate."

"My mom has a cold too." Debbie made room on the table for the board.

"'Tis the season." Janet lifted the board higher. "I made this before Mom called to cancel—so I was happy to have it all ready when you called."

"Thank you." Debbie motioned toward the table. "Hot chocolate? Tea? Coffee?"

"How about coffee?" Ian asked.

"Just water for me," Janet said.

"Back in a flash," Debbie said.

"I'll help." Janet followed her into the kitchen, closed the door, and said to Debbie, "There's a ring box on the table."

"I'm aware," Debbie said. "It was Greg's grandmother's ring."

"What's he doing with it?"

"It showed up on his porch yesterday."

Janet's eyebrows raised. "That's...unusual. Are you sure that's *all* he's doing with it?"

Debbie laughed. "Positive." She knew what Janet was getting at.

It wasn't that Greg and Debbie hadn't talked *around* getting married, but she still didn't want to get her hopes up that he'd propose anytime soon. She hadn't entirely thought through whether she was ready for that kind of step.

A few minutes later, all four sat at the table as Greg explained what had happened.

"So this is all about a ring that's been found, not one that was stolen." Ian speared a piece of prosciutto with a wooden pick.

"Well, it did disappear thirty years ago, according to Aunt Sally," Greg said. "And Debbie accidentally found it—we weren't looking for it. It just showed up."

Debbie added, "We're hoping you can give us some advice to help us figure out who might have planted it in the box on the porch."

Ian leaned back in his chair. "Do you think the same person who somehow acquired the ring in the past put it in the box yesterday?"

"Maybe," Greg answered.

"That seems like the logical place to start," Debbie said.

Ian smiled. "Well, that narrows down the age of the suspect, doesn't it?"

Greg laughed and told him that Sally suspected his father took the ring. "She also said that their mother intended it to go to her."

"If your grandmother was forgetful before she passed away, she might have told Sally that she wanted her to have the ring. But then gave it to EJ for whatever reason. There's no evidence it was stolen. The only 'suspects'"—he made air quotes "—are relatives who might have each thought she wanted them to have it."

"That's good insight," Greg said. "Except Sally is speculating that Dad took it. Yet there's absolutely no evidence it was ever in his possession."

"Then we should concentrate on how the ring ended up in the box on your porch and who put it there."

Janet asked, "What motive could someone have to return the ring?"

"Perhaps they want to sell it," Ian said, "but don't want anyone finding out that they had it in the first place. Once they put it in the box and Greg found it and alerted people, they could claim they had rightful ownership."

"But why go to all that trouble? Why not just go sell it in another town?" Janet said. "How would anyone here know?"

"Perhaps it's a famous ring." Debbie picked a piece of cheese off the charcuterie board. "Maybe word would get out. Sally said it came from her father. He came by it in North Africa during the war, and then Ted Johnston—"

Greg added, "My step-grandfather—"

Debbie laid her hand on Greg's arm. "You should tell the story."

"Sally says Ted brought the ring, the knitting project, and a packet of letters back from Europe. He carried them in his backpack after Grandpa Earl died."

"Interesting." Ian cocked his head. "How old was Sally when Ted came to Dennison with the ring and scarf?"

Greg thought for a moment. "She was born in 1938."

"So eight," Debbie added, doing the math in her head.

Janet wrapped her hands around her mug. "Kids can certainly know what's going on at that age."

Ian asked, "How did she seem when all of you were talking about the ring?"

"Eager to blame Dad," Greg said. He sighed. "And then a little defensive."

Debbie kept her expression neutral. She'd thought so too, but she'd just met Sally. She didn't know what was normal for Greg's aunt.

Ian paused a moment and then asked Greg, "What about your mom? Perhaps she recently discovered it in your dad's things and wants to protect him."

Greg shook his head. "She says she'd never seen the ring or the knitting project before. She said Dad never mentioned them."

Janet cleared her throat. "We can trust Paulette on this. None of us have ever known Paulette to lie or be even a little shady." She laughed. "And I'm not just saying that because she's your mom."

Debbie agreed. There wasn't anyone more trustworthy than Paulette. Except for Greg.

"Mom wasn't faking being offended that Sally would accuse Dad," Greg said. "She was genuinely upset."

When they ran out of scenarios, the conversation shifted to the snow. Then Ian's phone buzzed with a text. He read it and said, "I've got to go. I'm in the middle of a case, and there's been a development."

After Janet and Ian left, Greg said, "I should get going too. Jaxon's been lax on his geometry homework. I need to make sure he's got it done."

Debbie walked with him to the front door. "Call me later if you want to talk about this more."

"All right."

As Greg put on his coat, Debbie asked, "What do you know about Katherine Johnston?"

"Not much."

"Where's she from?"

"Chicago, I think," Greg said. "That's where Ted was from."

"Like your mom said, it seems coincidental that she showed up asking about heirlooms right before the ring disappeared."

Greg zipped his coat. "It does. And Mom said last week, when she mentioned Katherine had stopped by, that she hadn't seen her for twenty years at least."

CHAPTER THREE

Monday, after the lunch rush, Debbie and Janet sat down at the back table with cups of coffee and samples of pastries Janet had made for the upcoming dance.

"What is this?" Debbie picked up a small heart-shaped treat.

"A chocolate hand pie."

Debbie took a bite, chewed, and swallowed. "So it's chocolate pie crust with chocolate in the middle?"

Janet nodded. "It's a ganache filling."

Debbie took a second, then a final bite. Each time, the chocolate inside burst out of the crust. "Wow. That was amazing."

"Thank you." Janet pointed to the bar in the middle. "Try this one—it's raspberry cheesecake."

Debbie took a taste. "That was delicious too." She took a sip of coffee. "I need to cleanse my palate."

Janet laughed. "Try a truffle when you're done with that."

"I'd better pace myself," Debbie said. "I'll try more this afternoon. Having a best friend who's an amazing baker is both a blessing and a curse."

Paulette stepped to the table. "But mostly a blessing, right?"

"Definitely," Debbie said.

Janet smiled at Paulette. "Sit down with Debbie." Janet stood. "And try a few samples. Let me know your favorites."

Paulette took Janet's place and picked up a chocolate truffle.

Debbie finished the cheesecake bar. "I have a question for you. Sally seemed adamant that Katherine Johnston wasn't looking for a ring. Are you as sure?"

"Yum. That was superb." Paulette wiped her fingers on a napkin and then shrugged. "I have no idea what exactly Katherine was looking for, but I'm kind of surprised Sally was so sure Katherine wasn't looking for the ring. Katherine acted like I knew exactly what she was talking about." She took a bite of the truffle.

Debbie smiled, hoping to encourage her to keep talking. Paulette picked up one of the hand pies and said, "Apparently she spoke with Sally before she talked with me, but Sally was in the middle of moving. Katherine said Sally cut the conversation short. She seemed to be convinced that some Johnston family heirlooms might have ended up with Ted's kids, or stepkids."

"But she didn't say what sort of heirlooms?"

"That's right. She stopped by the house right after I'd gotten home from the storage unit. I told her I was getting a couple of boxes of Vivian's things ready for Greg." She took a bite of the hand pie, and her eyes brightened. "How does Janet come up with these masterpieces?"

"Right? She's amazing." After a pause, Debbie asked, "Was looking for heirlooms the only reason Katherine was in town?"

"I don't think so," Paulette said. "She was staying with a third cousin in Uhrichsville who I've only met once. Katherine may have gone back to Chicago, but I'm not sure."

"Do you think it's a coincidence that Katherine appeared right before the ring turned up?"

"It does seem odd."

"Did you tell her you'd come from the storage unit?"

Paulette thought for a moment. "Yes, I believe I did."

"How old is Katherine?"

"Still in her seventies, I think. Probably late seventies, maybe early eighties. She's younger than Sally—and a few years younger than EJ would have been. Sally told me in the car on the way home that Katherine was always in everybody's business, even when they were kids."

Debbie chuckled. "Do you mind sharing Sally's phone number with me? I'd like to pick her brain a little more. If she'll let me."

Paulette gave her the number and then stood. "I should head out. I need to run a few errands."

Debbie rose and gave Paulette a hug. "See you tomorrow."

Once Paulette left, Debbie returned to the kitchen.

"You two looked pretty serious. Is there a new lead as far as the ring?" Janet scraped the grill as she talked.

"Well, I don't think I mentioned this last night. But a cousin was in town last week asking Sally and Paulette about family heirlooms."

"I've been thinking. What if Sally is mistaken? We know how family stories get changed over time, like a game of telephone. What if the ring wasn't from Earl? If it was from Ted, it could be one of his family's heirlooms."

"But why would Ted give it to Vivian the first day he met her? That makes little sense."

"Maybe Sally is mistaken about that too." Janet poured clean oil on the grill. "Yesterday, I assumed she remembered things correctly. But maybe not. Maybe the ring didn't get carried all over wartime Europe with the letters. Maybe Ted gave Vivian the yarn and scarf right away—for whatever reason—and then gave her the ring later." Janet paused a moment. "Then again, maybe the ring wasn't from Ted *or* from Earl. Maybe it was an heirloom from Vivian's own family."

"That's a thought," Debbie said. "Vivian was born in England. I believe her mother's first husband, who died fairly young, was wealthy."

Janet began scrubbing the grill. She turned her head toward Debbie as she spoke. "Would it be helpful if I look into all the families?"

"Yes," Debbie said. "The Connors and Johnstons, for sure. Vivian's maiden name was Olson, but I'll need to ask Greg about anything further back and text you the information."

"Great!" Janet stood. "Have you started a suspect list?"

Debbie shook her head.

"You should. Be sure to add the cousin from Chicago."

At closing time, Greg came into the café, appearing a little harried as the last customer left. Debbie turned the sign then said, "Is everything all right?"

"No." Greg ran his hand through his hair.

Alarmed, Debbie asked, "What happened? Are the boys okay?"

His face lightened. "The boys are fine. It's nothing like that. I mean it's the reverse of that."

"What are you talking about?" Debbie asked, completely confused.

"The ring."

Oh no. Had he lost it? "Did something happen?"

·"Nothing. I mean I had it looked at. Appraised."

"And?"

"It's definitely worth something. A lot."

Debbie gasped. "What?"

"Yes. That's what the jeweler said. But he also said I should get a professional appraisal from a gemologist. In the meantime, he said to keep it in a safe place."

"Wow."

Greg sat down at the counter. "Why would my humble grandmother own a ring like that?"

Debbie shook her head. "A valuable ring that she kept in the middle of a ball of yarn."

Greg grinned. "It's ludicrous. And frankly, I'm going to hold off getting too excited until I have it evaluated by the gemologist."

"All the more reason to figure out where it came from, though. I mean, if it really was valuable, it must have had a lot of sentimental value for her not to sell it at some point."

Greg interjected, "Or maybe she had no idea how much it was worth."

"Sally said she knew it was worth something. But then again, everybody has a different understanding of what 'worth something' means." Debbie sat down beside him. "Where's the ring now?"

"My safe deposit box at the bank."

"Good idea," she said. "What do you plan to tell your mom and Sally?"

Greg clasped her hand and gave it a squeeze. His felt warm and strong in hers. She was so grateful to have him in her life.

"The truth. That I need to take it to a gemologist. Thank you for helping me with this."

"Of course," Debbie said. "We'll find out where the ring came from."

"And then we need to find out who it belongs to now," Greg answered. "I'm hoping you'll find some clues in Grandma's diaries or letters."

Greg retrieved his phone from his pocket with his free hand. "I should call Sally." After he placed the call, he put it on speaker and set it on the counter.

"Hi, Greg." Sally sounded pleasant. "Did you get the ring appraised?"

"Hello to you too." Greg laughed. "I'm with Debbie and have you on speaker. As to your question, not exactly. The jeweler suggested I take it to a gemologist."

"See, I was right," Sally said. "It *is* worth something. You'll see that I'm right about all of it. That it was from Daddy for Mama. That Ted brought it to her. That it was intended to be passed down to me."

Debbie couldn't help but smile. Sally was assertive, and she liked that about her. The woman had firm convictions.

"Let me know how much it's worth," Sally said. "And then we can talk."

Greg smiled and said, "I will."

Debbie quickly added, "I was wondering if you could give me Katherine's phone number."

"What do you want to ask her?"

"Paulette said she was asking about Johnston family heirlooms last week. I wanted more information about what she was looking for."

"Why?"

"Well, I'm trying to help Greg figure out where the ring came from and who put it in his box," Debbie answered. "Katherine seems like someone we ought to talk to."

Sally chuckled. "Talking with Katherine will be a rabbit trail, but I won't prevent you from going down it." She rattled off a number, seemingly from memory.

"Hold on," Debbie said. "Let me get a pen."

Debbie barely had one in her hand when Sally rattled off the number again. Then she said, "Remember, Greg, let me know as soon as you have a dollar amount on the ring. Bye."

After Debbie left the café, she hurried to her car. More snow fell, adding to the foot that had already accumulated over the last three days. The temperatures continued to be well below freezing and down to around twenty during the night. It wouldn't be melting anytime soon.

Once she reached her home, turned up the heat, and sat in the living room with a cup of tea, she pulled out her phone and dialed Katherine's number. No one answered. Debbie left a message, explaining who she was and that she'd like to ask Katherine a few questions either in person or over the phone.

After she hung up, she thought through her evening. She'd made chicken tortellini soup the evening before, after Greg left, and had leftovers. She needed to do some grocery shopping. Did she want to go out now? Not really, but she should get it done.

She thought of her parents and texted to see if they needed anything from the store. THANK YOU, BUT WE'RE FINE, her mother responded. Next, she thought of her friends Ray and Eileen at Good Shepherd and wondered if she could pick up anything for them. Perhaps Sally needed items too. She called Ray. He requested a tube of toothpaste. Next she called Eileen, who said she needed a box of tissues. Then she texted Sally, who texted back a nine-item list that included a bag of popcorn, chocolate chips, nail polish remover, and hand lotion.

Debbie laughed. Sally knew what she needed.

An hour later, Debbie stepped into the lobby of Good Shepherd. Ray was in his wheelchair next to Eileen, who sat in a chair, while Sally sat across from them on the love seat.

Debbie beamed. "I'm so glad the three of you have already met."

Eileen gave her a puzzled look.

Sally said, "I just sat down."

"Oh," Debbie said. "Eileen and Ray, I'd like you to meet Greg's aunt, Sally Watts. Sally, this is Eileen Palmer and Ray Zink."

"Pleased to meet you," Sally said. "Although after giving both of you a second look, I realized I already know you."

"Sally Connor," Eileen said. "Of course. Your grandpa Olson worked for the railroad."

"Yes," Sally said. "He did." She turned to Debbie. "In fact, my grandparents lived close to where you are now." She smiled at Ray. "Where you grew up. I thought about all of that after I left Debbie's last night."

Ray returned her smile. "You must have just moved in here, right?"

"Yes. On Saturday."

"Welcome," Eileen said.

Debbie pulled out Ray's toothpaste and Eileen's box of tissues and then handed the bag to Sally.

"Well, thank you," Sally said. "It's good to know I have support here."

"You do. Absolutely," Debbie said.

"With no ulterior motives?" Sally smirked.

"Pardon?" Was Sally accusing her of being duplicitous?

"It seems you and Greg are rather serious."

Debbie's face grew warm. What was Sally getting at?

"I'm thinking a ring is in your future."

"That will be news to me," Debbie said. "And, with all due respect, it's not anything that's open for discussion."

"What do we owe you?" Ray asked.

After each paid Debbie, Sally pursed her lips. "Back to that ring…"

Ray turned to Eileen and said, "Would you push me into the dining hall?"

Eileen stood. "Certainly."

Ray asked, "Sally, would you join us for dinner?"

"I'd like that," she said.

"How about you, Debbie?" Ray asked. "Will you join us too?"

Debbie stood. "Another time. I think I'd better go on home. I have quite a bit I need to get done tonight, and I have groceries."

"Thank you so much, dear." Eileen grasped the back of Ray's chair.

"Yes, thank you." Ray twinkled up at Debbie with his still-vibrant blue eyes.

Sally held up her bag of items and chirped, "Thanks!" She turned toward the hallway and said to Eileen and Ray, "See you in a few."

As Debbie left Good Shepherd, she wondered if Sally had always been so cavalier and outspoken. Or was this more recent behavior?

For Greg's sake, she would be tolerant and understanding of the woman. Even if she had all but accused Debbie of wanting her mother's antique for an engagement ring.

An hour later, after she put away her groceries and ate leftover soup in the kitchen, Debbie sat down at the dining room table. She placed the stacks of letters on her right side and the stack of diaries on the other. The first diary entry was July 29, 1938.

> *Today, I've become a mother. Sarah Rose Connor was born this morning at 5:32. Earl and I are over the moon. I only wish Daisy could be here to hold her little niece, who we'll call Sally.*

Interesting that Vivian had mentioned her sister Daisy in her first entry. Debbie recalled that Greg had not even been aware Vivian had a sister, but this seemed to prove it. Where was Daisy in 1938?

I'm brimming with love for this little one and for Earl too. Earl sent word to Mum, who said she will visit once we are home. Daddy is in Chicago for work. At least Mum isn't waiting until our next planned Sunday dinner in the middle of August to see her first grandchild.

Will and Mary have come already to meet our little Sally right away. Earl's parents are nearly as enchanted with her as we are. I'm very grateful to the Lord for this little one and pray for more. I want at least a dozen altogether, and Earl agrees. Our old farmhouse has six bedrooms, although the upstairs ones need a lot of work. Even so, we have the room and the desire. Growing up with only one sister ten years older than me makes me want to fill this house with love and laughter.

The next entry was a month later.

Caring for a baby is taking far more time than I expected, along with seeing to the house and cooking three meals a day, plus tending the garden and helping Earl with the farm as I can. Harvest has started, which means Earl is in the fields from dawn to dusk, with only a few minutes for lunch. I've had a letter of congratulations from Daisy. Of course, she is thrilled with the news of Sally and requested a photograph right away. She sent a bit of money to put away for her. Daisy wrote she spent her usual holiday in the French Riviera with her Dumont grandparents, aunts, uncles, and cousins, writing that all of them are leery of what Hitler might do next.

Debbie paused, noting that Vivian had written "*her* Dumont grandparents…" not *our*. Did Daisy and Vivian have different fathers? She continued reading.

She invited Sally and me to England. She said she'll cover our expenses, and we would stay in the London flat for a few days and then go to Noel's family's country home.

I'm tempted, but with the travel we'd be gone six weeks. I can't bear to be away from Earl for that long. And I don't think it prudent to take Sally on such a long trip at such a young age.

I'm afraid Daisy will need to come here if we're to visit. I'll write her back and see if she will.

Debbie found the letter from Daisy, with the return address of Mrs. Noel Chapman. So Noel was her husband. Debbie returned to skimming through the diary entries. On September 1, 1939, Germany invaded Poland, starting the war in Europe. In May of 1940, Vivian had another girl, Carol. In September of 1940, the Selective Training Service Act in the US required men between twenty-one and forty-five to register for the draft. That same month, Germany began bombing the UK. Daisy hadn't visited, and of course Vivian hadn't traveled to England. Noel, who had served in the Navy after the Great War, was commissioned as an officer and sent to the South Pacific.

A letter from Daisy described the London Blitz, saying she was safe and her flat near Hyde Park hadn't been hit. She added at the end, almost as an afterthought, that she'd been driving an ambulance in London and hadn't been to Noel's family's country home for months. Vivian wrote in her journal that she prayed for her sister every day.

In May of 1941, she wrote that the Blitz ended, although some bombing continued. Daisy had survived! But then in August a letter arrived from Daisy, saying that German bombs had obliterated her flat.

It's all gone. All of our childhood memories blown to smithereens. Thankfully, I made it to the Underground before the bomb hit. I'll go to the country for now and decide what to do.

With every word Debbie read, she became more and more enthralled with the story.

CHAPTER FOUR

Connor Farm, Dennison, Ohio
December 8, 1941

Vivian sat in the living room of their farmhouse, rocking the baby. Carol was a year and a half, but something had awakened her in the night. Perhaps an earache to go with the cold she'd come down with the day before. Perhaps it was the tensions of the afternoon and evening. The Japanese had bombed Pearl Harbor. The United States was at war on one front and would likely soon be at war with Germany too.

Little Carol stopped crying and finally settled against Vivian's chest. In another minute the baby's breathing changed. Vivian kissed the top of her second daughter's head. Would Earl be drafted? Would their idyllic life on their farm in the rolling hills of Ohio change forever?

She breathed a prayer that the Lord would give her strength whatever might come. She must have dozed in the chair, because she awoke to Earl standing over her. He whispered, "I'll take the baby. Go get another hour of sleep."

He reached down and lifted the little one into his arms. All she'd ever wanted was a good man to share her life with and a houseful of children. Even when she lived in the London flat with Mum, Daddy, and Daisy, that's what she wanted. To live on a farm. To work alongside her husband. To raise a big family. In three months, her third baby would arrive. Would Earl still be on the farm? Or would he be far, far away? When she realized she was expecting again, she told him they were on their way to a dozen children. She'd teased, "At this rate, we'll still be young when the last one arrives." What would the war mean for her lifelong dreams?

She awoke to the light coming through the bedroom curtains. The smell of bacon enticed her out of bed. She slipped into her robe, cinching it above her expanding waistline, and headed for the kitchen. Carol sat in the high chair Earl had made, and Sally sat at the table, a piece of bread in her hand.

"Good morning, sweetheart," Earl called out from the stove.

Tears pricked Vivian's eyes. She'd never been happier. Perhaps the threat of war made her even more aware of this beautiful life she had.

Three days later Germany declared war on the United States.

The next Sunday at church, there was a notice in the bulletin about a knitting circle forming to help supply soldiers with warm clothing—sweaters, socks, mufflers, and fingerless mitts. Do your bit for the war effort! *the notice concluded.*

Earl pointed to the notice in his bulletin as Vivian finished reading hers and then whispered, "Would you like to do this?"

Vivian shook her head. She had no one to watch the girls, and it would take away from her work on the farm. But as the service started, she thought about it more. She enjoyed knitting, although she didn't have time to do it much anymore except for necessities such as socks for her family.

Daisy, older than Vivian by a decade, had taught her to knit when she was eight. Sometimes in the evening, usually in the dreary winter, they'd sit by the fire in Daisy's room in their London flat and knit. Vivian had started with a scarf but soon mastered making mittens and socks and then sweaters. She'd enjoyed that time with her sister.

But she knew her mother wouldn't watch the girls to allow Vivian to join the knitting circle. Not that Mum didn't love her granddaughters—she just didn't want to spend much time with them.

Earl gave her a questioning look. She shook her head again.

"I'll care for the girls. It's during nap time," he whispered. "I'll work on my books while they sleep."

When she arrived at the church on Wednesday afternoon, thirteen women had already gathered. Most were older than Vivian. She knew several of them and recognized the rest. The pastor's wife, Martha Wilkinson, welcomed everyone, then said, "My brother-in-law works for the Red Cross in Columbus and connected me with the knitting program that started in September. Now, with us at war, the need will multiply." She motioned to the table beside her, which was covered with patterns and yarn. "The Red Cross has supplied patterns for our work, along with olive and navy blue yarn."

An elderly woman with her gray hair tucked under a scarf asked, "How often will we meet?"

"Once a week, on Wednesday afternoons. I know that's a lot to ask, and I realize all of you won't be able to come to every meeting, but please come as often as you can. 'Knit your bit' is the rallying cry, and it's

a genuine need. These items will keep our soldiers, sailors, and marines warm. We can hope this war will soon be over, but every item you knit for a serviceman will help the United States win."

Vivian shivered, and not from the drafty church hall. That's what they all wanted. To win the war as soon as possible.

Martha smiled. "Of course, next Wednesday is Christmas Eve, so we won't meet then or on New Year's Eve. We'll start back up on January 7th. So take extra patterns and yarn to knit in case you have time over the holidays."

The navy blue items would go to sailors in the Pacific. The soldiers wearing the olive items would head to Europe. Vivian chose a sleeveless sweater pattern and the drab olive yarn, thinking of her sister in England. She would knit something for a soldier first.

The women sat at tables with the patterns laid out around them. The elderly woman with the scarf tied around her head introduced herself as Blanche and then asked Vivian how long she'd lived in Dennison.

"Six years," she answered. "The Pennsylvania Railroad transferred my father here in 1935. I graduated high school in 1936."

Blanche gave Vivian a questioning look. "Do I detect a hint of an accent?"

Vivian's face grew warm. It had been years since anyone had mentioned an accent. She tried so hard when she arrived in Philadelphia in 1927 as a ten-year-old to emulate the way the other children spoke. And then again when her father was transferred to Pittsburgh. And through all of her father's other transfers. "I was born in London," Vivian said. "My father is American though, and I've been here for most of my life."

"Do you have kinfolk still in England?" another woman asked.

Vivian nodded. "A sister and brother-in-law, although he's serving in Asia now."

"How were things for your sister during the Blitz?"

"All right," Vivian answered. "She drove an ambulance. But her apartment was bombed in July. Thankfully she was sheltering in the Underground at the time."

"Goodness." Blanche peered over her glasses. "She must be a brave woman."

Vivian swallowed the lump in her throat and said, "Yes. She is." Daisy had always been brave. Now she was on her own in England while Noel was off at war.

When Christmas Eve arrived, Earl, Vivian, and the children spent time with Earl's parents and then had a formal dinner on Christmas Day with Vivian's.

Mum had prepared a roast with vegetables and bread pudding for dessert. But halfway through the meal, the phone rang. Daddy excused himself and headed to the hall. A few minutes later, he returned with his hat and overcoat. "I'm afraid I've been called away. There's a problem with the track this side of Pittsburgh," he said. His hazel eyes were bright as he glanced around the table. "Merry Christmas to all of you."

The conversation lulled for a moment, but then Vivian thought of the knitting circle and told Mum about it.

Mum patted her twisted hair at the back of her neck. "That's lovely, dear."

"I've made a sleeveless sweater so far and am nearly done with a scarf," Vivian said. "Would you like to come with me to the next one? It starts up again after the holidays."

"Thank you for the invitation." Mum smiled. "I'll give it some thought."

Vivian smiled in return. "I think of Daisy all the time, but especially while I'm knitting."

Mum's face hardened. She opened her mouth to respond, but before she could, Sally knocked over her milk, splashing it across Mum's lace tablecloth. Vivian gasped as she stood and quickly righted the glass.

Milk dripped down Sally's legs and onto the floor. Using her cloth napkin, Vivian stopped the flow.

"Goodness." Mum fixed her gaze on Sally. "Was that necessary?"

During the month of January, Vivian knitted another sleeveless sweater, three scarves, several pairs of fingerless gloves, and two pairs of socks, all during the evenings while listening to the radio after the girls went to bed. When the news came on, Vivian practically held her breath. By the first week of January, more than 100,000 men had volunteered for the military, and more and more were being drafted and sent away for training. The baby growing inside her kicked more when she was knitting, probably because it was the only time during the day when Vivian sat still.

In early March, Earl brought in the mail as she readied to go into town for the knitting circle. Carol had fussed at going down for her nap, causing Vivian to run late.

Earl held out an envelope. "You have a letter from Daisy."

Vivian took it and slipped it into her purse. She'd take a minute to read it in quiet before she headed home after the knitting circle.

She sat by Blanche, the older woman she'd met the first day. "How long until your baby is due?" the woman asked.

"A month." Vivian glanced down at her pattern.

"And you have two little ones at home?"

"Yes." Vivian met Blanche's gaze. "Sally is four, and Carol turned two last month."

"I had my children close together too," Blanche said. "Seven in twelve years. A big family is a lot of work—but worth it." She winked. "In the long run."

Vivian couldn't help but chuckle. "We want a big family too."

After the knitting circle ended, Vivian sat in the truck in the church parking lot and opened Daisy's letter. Tears stung as she read. Noel had been killed in the Battle of Singapore in February.

Would you please tell Mummy and your father? I can't bring myself to write another letter with the bad news at the moment.

I don't have much news other than that. I haven't heard from my grandparents in Paris since last November.

She hoped they were at their chateau in Normandy. She continued reading Daisy's letter.

I'm glad to hear you're knitting and helping that way. Has Earl been drafted yet? I hate to think of him leaving you and your babies, but if we don't have the help of the US soon, I'm not sure what will happen to England, let alone France and the rest of Europe. We certainly are in a horrible mess. We must all do our part to right our world as soon as possible. The losses will be even more dire if we don't.

Daisy had certainly done her part. She'd driven an ambulance. Lost her flat. Lost her husband without a word of complaint. Lost contact, mostly, with her French family.

Vivian shivered. She doubted she'd be as graceful as her big sister if the same happened to her.

Kiss your babies for me. Visit Mother and be patient with her, please. I know how difficult she can be, but it's her nervous state, more than anything. She doesn't do it on purpose. Please tell her how much I love and miss her.

Vivian put the letter back into her purse, started the truck, and headed toward her parents' house near the depot. When the railroad transferred Daddy to Dennison in 1935, Vivian guessed it would only be for a year or two. Mum was surprised by how small the town was after having lived in London and then Philadelphia, Pittsburgh, Cleveland, and Chicago. But Dennison was a crossroads for trains going every which way in the vast nation of the United States. Now, with the war effort escalating, even more trains came through the town each day, and Daddy's job was more important than ever.

As Vivian pulled the truck to the curb in front of the house, she noted Daddy's Buick in the driveway. Most likely he'd walked to the depot that day. It was only a few blocks. Or perhaps he was working out of town.

She knocked on the front door. When no one answered, she tried the knob. It was unlocked. "Hello," she called out. "It's Vivian."

No one answered. Then she heard footsteps. Daddy's. He came through the door to the kitchen into the dining room. "Vivian," he said. "What are you doing here?"

"I have bad news," she answered.

Daddy's brows knitted together. "What is it?"

"I had a letter from Daisy. Noel was killed in the Battle of Singapore."

He rubbed his forehead. "Your mother is having a bad day, but it won't do any good to keep this information from her."

Vivian agreed. "Daisy asked me to tell her. She thought it would be better than sending the news in a letter."

"Wait in the living room. I'll see if she is up to a visit."

Alarmed, Vivian asked, "Is she ill?"

"Somewhat. She's been having headaches. Fatigue. That sort of thing."

Vivian had no idea her mother hadn't been well. She'd been so busy with the farm and Earl and the girls. As her father left the room, she sat down in the chair by the fireplace. About ten minutes later, Daddy led Mum into the room. Mum greeted Vivian with a kiss on the cheek and then sat on the sofa. Daddy stood.

"Charlotte," he said. "Vivian has had a letter from Daisy. Noel's been killed in the South Pacific."

Mum turned to Vivian. "Why didn't she write me?"

Daddy spoke before Vivian could answer. "How is Daisy doing?"

"Holding up, it seems." Vivian leaned back in the chair. Daisy actually hadn't said how she was doing. "Mum, she told me to tell you how much she loves and misses you."

Mum brushed away a tear.

"I wish she would come to the US," Daddy said.

"So do I," Vivian answered.

Mum stood. "Well, I know you need to get back to the children. I'm going to go rest. I've had a headache all week."

Vivian stood too. "Have you seen the doctor—"

"When is your baby due?" Mum crossed her arms. "I've forgotten."

Vivian clasped her hands together. "In a month."

Mum shook her head. "Why aren't you home resting?"

Vivian didn't respond.

Daddy made to follow Mum but paused and said to Vivian, "Do you have a few more minutes? I will walk you out."

She answered, "I'll wait outside."

The day had grown colder, and dark clouds gathered on the horizon. Vivian shivered and fastened the top buttons of her coat. After ten minutes she climbed in the truck to get out of the chill. What was keeping him?

Finally Daddy came out of the house with his coat and hat on. She waved. He began walking toward her.

He opened the door and asked, "Mind if I sit for a moment?"

She was anxious to get home so Earl could do the afternoon chores before the rain started, but Daddy had something to tell her, and she feared she needed to hear it.

"You and Earl are good parents," he said. "I'm glad there will be another baby."

Vivian hadn't expected that, but the sentiment pleased her. "How long has Mum been ill?"

"She's been having headaches off and on for months. The doctor says it's nerves, it seems from the war. She's heartsick about what's happened to London and all of England. Worried about Daisy. Worried about what will happen to you and the girls if Earl is drafted."

Vivian would never have guessed her mother was worried about her. "She doesn't act as if she's worried. She acts angry."

"That's how some people show it. The doctor said she needs rest but also social interaction. And good food."

Vivian put her hands on the steering wheel. "Is she getting those things?"

"Some," Daddy answered. "I've hired a woman to come in every morning to help with the housework and to make a meal. I'm trying not to travel more than necessary."

"How can I help with Mum?" Vivian asked.

"Well, I don't expect anything now. But after you recover from your confinement, could you stop by more often? Perhaps after your knitting circle every week if you continue with that? Even if it's just for a half hour."

"Yes, of course." Vivian hoped Mum would want to see her.

"I wish she'd go with you to the knitting circle," Daddy said. "But she says she's not interested."

"Perhaps the focus on the war wouldn't be helpful."

"That could be." Daddy opened the car door. "I need to be on my way. Please tell Earl hello."

Vivian nodded. "I will."

Daddy climbed down and stood on the sidewalk, facing her. "I'm proud of you, Vivian. You've made a good life for yourself here."

On the drive home, the tears began to flow. Noel had been eleven years older than Daisy, tall and handsome. Daisy was petite and vivacious. Vivian had only been ten when the two married. Daisy's father, Mum's first husband, had been from a wealthy French family, whom Daisy stayed close to after he died. Her grandparents, who owned a textile company in France, had paid for the wedding and invited their wealthy friends, while Noel's family—who had a manor house in Berkshire—had invited their aristocratic friends.

It had been a fairy-tale wedding on the grounds of Daisy's grandparents' chateau on the outskirts of the village of Saint-Vaast-la-Hougue. Vivian had feared that she and Mum and Daddy would seem out of place, but Daisy's grandparents had been welcoming and kind. They seemed to adore Mum—their once daughter-in-law—and they absolutely loved Daisy. But who didn't? Vivian's big sister was kind, funny, and beautiful. She lit up every room she entered, and she absolutely shone as a bride. Noel was truly smitten by her. Everyone was.

It had been a glorious day. But now that had all changed for Daisy. Vivian could only wonder what changes were ahead for her too.

CHAPTER FIVE

Tuesday morning, Debbie stood at her upstairs bedroom window. The streetlights cast a soft glow over the snow, making for a magical scene. She said a silent prayer of thanks for the enchanting world outside, and for the warm, though drafty, bungalow she could call her own. More snow had fallen during the night, but thankfully the city plow had already gone by.

As Debbie got ready for work, she thought of Vivian and what she knew of the woman. Born in England, she navigated her early adulthood as a mother and wife during one of the most tumultuous times in history. With four young children, she'd lost her first husband to war. Then she remarried and had three more kids. In time, the children grew up and mostly lived elsewhere. But that's what children did. Only Sally and EJ stayed in Ohio.

Debbie could tell, from Greg's stories, that Vivian had been the cornerstone of the family. As she had begun to read Vivian's diary and her letters last night, Debbie dreaded what was to come in later pages. She knew the ending for Earl, and it was heartbreaking, bringing back memories of the loss of her own fiancé, Reed, who'd been killed in Afghanistan. But at least Vivian had found love again and made a good life for herself with Ted Johnston. Until she was widowed a second time.

As Debbie stood at the dining room, placing a stack of Vivian's photographs into her bag to take to the depot to show Kim, Greg called. She knew the boys would still be asleep, but Greg was an early riser like her.

"What are you up to?" he asked.

"I was thinking about your grandmother." She told him what she'd learned from what she'd read so far.

"Fascinating," Greg said. "I've been thinking about her a lot too and trying to recall as many memories of her as I can."

"What are some of the highlights?"

"Holiday dinners at the farm, before Grandpa Ted died. By then, Aunt Sally and Mom did most of the cooking, but Grandma was always in the kitchen, helping wherever she could. Brant and I would spend most of our time outside. Grandma would send us out with scraps for the chickens or a basket to collect eggs. She kept us busy with chores. 'Be productive,' she'd say, and 'Many hands make light work.' A few times there was a calf that needed to be bottle-fed. That was always my favorite. After Grandpa Ted passed away, Grandma would say the blessing when we gathered as a family. It was always a short and sweet prayer, but it made me feel warm inside. She made me feel as if I belonged."

Debbie said, "You did."

"Yeah. But you know how some older people only tolerate kids? I always felt as if she cherished them."

"That's so sweet." Debbie thought of Vivian wanting a dozen children. It seemed her wish was genuine, even if she'd fallen a few short of that number. "What do you remember about her last days?"

56

"By then she appeared so small in the hospital bed Dad set up in the living room of the farmhouse. She was probably a little over five and a half feet or so and had always been strong, but the cancer took so much from her. She was thin and frail at the end. Sally, Dad, and Mom all helped care for her. I was fourteen, so I was pretty aware of what was going on. Dad was heartbroken. I was too. We all were. But I figured she was old, and it was her time, but now, looking back, I realize that seventy-five wasn't that old at all. Dad had probably expected to have his mother around for another decade or more." He paused a moment and said, "I get that, now that Mom is getting close to that age."

Debbie thought the same about her parents. She hoped they'd live another couple of decades too.

"Grandma was Dad's hero. Or heroine, I should say. She might not have fought in a war, but she fought for the home front her entire life."

Debbie liked that. Perhaps she and Kim could work that idea into the title of the exhibit. Maybe *Fighting for the Home Front*. She'd talk to Kim about it.

After she said goodbye to Greg, Debbie texted her mother. How ARE YOU FEELING?

BETTER, her mother replied. DEFINITELY ON THE MEND, THOUGH I'M GOING TO TAKE IT EASY FOR ANOTHER COUPLE DAYS SO I DON'T SHARE THIS WITH ANYONE. I MISS YOU AND LOVE YOU!

Debbie responded with three hearts and then, I LOVE YOU TOO!

The café hummed all morning long. More snow didn't seem to be slowing anyone down—in fact, Debbie guessed people were making an extra effort to get out and enjoy it. It wasn't until ten thirty that business slowed enough for Debbie and Janet to sit at the back table and take a break.

Janet had brought along another plate of samples. As Debbie tried a chocolate peanut butter cheesecake bar, Janet said, "I did some research on the Connor family last night."

Debbie swallowed. "And?"

"Earl Sr.'s parents, William and Mary, married in Pittsburgh, Pennsylvania, in 1910. He worked for the railroad as a switchman, and he was transferred to New Philadelphia, Ohio by 1915." Janet tried a sample of the peanut butter bar herself before continuing. "Earl was born in 1917. His parents bought a property in 1923 about a mile from where he and Vivian eventually bought their farm. He had no siblings."

Debbie's heart lurched. "Will and Mary Connor ended up losing their only child. I can't imagine."

Janet agreed. "They must have really treasured their grandchildren."

"And Vivian," Debbie added. "I wonder about their relationship with Ted."

Janet took a sip of coffee, then in a contemplative voice said, "I hope it was good. He couldn't replace their son—but it seems he was a good father to their grandchildren."

Debbie made a mental note to ask Greg what he knew or had heard about his great-grandparents.

That afternoon, after Debbie closed the café and finished the cleaning and prep work for the next day, she ventured out to the museum with the box of photographs to share with Kim for the exhibit.

A docent was speaking with visitors at the front of the museum. Debbie headed back to Kim's office and knocked on the door when she reached it.

"Come in," Kim said.

Debbie opened the door. "It's me."

Kim looked exhausted. But of course Debbie didn't say so. Instead she asked, "How is Barry? How are you?"

"They're doing more tests tomorrow morning," Kim said. "I won't be in until noon or so."

Debbie sat down in the chair across from Kim with the box in her lap. "How is Barry feeling?"

"The same. Short of breath. Fatigued. Some dizziness," Kim said. "They've done an EKG and initial labs. His labs were okay. He has a heart murmur, which he's known about, but there were irregularities with his EKG. I'm hoping further lab tests tomorrow will give us an answer."

"I hope so too." Debbie set the box on the desk in front of Kim.

"What do you have there?" Kim asked.

"Photos from World War II that belonged to Vivian."

Kim's face lit up, and she rubbed her hands together. "I'm all ears and eyes. This is just the kind of project I need to keep my mind off Barry."

Debbie lifted the lid. "First, I was wondering about titles. What do you think about 'Fighting for the Home Front'?"

"I like that. Or 'Knitting for the War Fronts.'"

Debbie smiled. "Funny you'd say that. There was an odd ball of yarn and the beginning of a scarf in Vivian's things. But Paulette says it wasn't initially with the boxes of things she had of Vivian's."

"Interesting. Did you bring the yarn and scarf?"

"No." Debbie put the box on the table. "But I've found information about Vivian and her knitting. She wrote in her diary about when she first learned—her older half sister Daisy taught her when she was young and still lived in England. She also wrote about the first knitting circle meetings she attended at the church."

"Oh, good." Kim tapped her fingers on her desk. "Any photographs of her knitting or knitting projects?"

"I haven't come across any. I can ask Sally—"

"I know Sally," Kim interrupted. "Mom said she's living at Good Shepherd."

"Yes. I saw your mom the other day."

"I'm not telling her Barry's having health problems. Not yet, until we know something concrete. I don't want her to worry."

"I didn't say anything—and won't." Debbie took out the photographs. "I'll leave you these. And I'll also ask Sally about photographs showing knitting. I'll compile a document of letter and diary excerpts once I've gone through everything."

"Thank you," Kim said. "See if Sally remembers anything else about Vivian's knitting project—I'm curious about the scarf."

"I will." Debbie handed the photos to Kim. "There are photos of Vivian and Earl when they were first married, on the farm, and with their two oldest daughters. I'll bring more as I go through everything." She stood. "I should get going."

For a second, Debbie considered telling Kim about the ring. But that should be up to Greg. "I'll bring in the scarf," Debbie said as she reached the door.

On the way home, as Debbie clomped through the snow, her phone dinged. It was Greg. I HAVE A FAVOR TO ASK. COULD YOU PICK UP THE BOYS FROM BASKETBALL PRACTICE? I HAVE A MEETING THAT A CLIENT RESCHEDULED FOR FIVE AND MOM ALREADY COMMITTED TO DINNER WITH SALLY.

NO PROBLEM, Debbie texted back. SHOULD WE GET A PIZZA ON THE WAY HOME?

THAT WOULD BE GREAT. WOULD YOU GRAB A SALAD TOO?

ABSOLUTELY. WE'LL LEAVE YOU LEFTOVERS—AT LEAST OF THE SALAD. ☺

Greg texted, HAHA. I'LL TEXT THE BOYS AND LET THEM KNOW TO LOOK FOR YOUR CAR. PARK OUTSIDE THE GYM, AND THEY'LL FIND YOU WHEN THEY COME OUT.

Debbie slipped her phone back into her pocket. She was happy to help Greg, and she appreciated every interaction she had with Julian and Jaxon. Julian had always been warm to her, and Jaxon was finally coming around.

The lowering sun cast a silvery hue across the white lawns and flocked trees. It was beautiful. Debbie picked up her pace as more snow fell.

An hour later, Debbie sat in her car in the school parking lot waiting for the boys. She scanned the other vehicles. She knew almost all the parents. Dating Greg had introduced her to an entire population of people in the Dennison-Uhrichsville area she'd otherwise not know.

The gymnasium door opened, and two boys she recognized from Julian's team stepped out. A couple of minutes later Julian appeared with three other boys. He saw Debbie, waved, said something to his friends, and then started jogging to her car.

He opened the front passenger door as he called out a "See you tomorrow!" to another friend. Then he collapsed into the front seat as he ran his hand through his wet hair. "Wow. What a practice."

"What happened?" Debbie asked, turning up the heat.

"Running lines. Lots of them."

"Are you ready for Friday's game?"

"No." He turned and grinned at her. "But we will be." He reached over and honked her horn. "There's Jaxon."

Jaxon stood outside the gym door, glancing around. Julian honked again as he lowered his window. "We're over here!"

His brother turned toward the car and began walking. Slowly. Julian groaned. Jaxon gave a slight wave to someone who called out his name as he reached the car. Then he slumped into the back seat.

Once he closed his door, Debbie said, "Hi, Jaxon. How was practice?"

"Fine." His seat belt clicked.

As Debbie backed out of the parking place, she said, "Pizza for dinner. I already called in for pepperoni and a salad. Does that sound good?"

"Yes!" Julian said as Jaxon answered, "I don't care."

Debbie glanced in the rearview mirror. Jaxon stared out his window with a blank expression on his face. Maybe he'd had a bad day at school. Or a bad practice.

As they pulled into the parking lot of the restaurant, Paulette came out carrying a pizza box.

"Grandma!" Julian opened his door as soon as Debbie parked next to Paulette's car.

"What are you doing here?" Paulette asked.

Julian climbed out, leaving the door open, and gave his grandmother a hug as she balanced the box in one hand. "Picking up a pizza. Same as you."

She laughed. "Your great-aunt Sally and I are going to eat it at Good Shepherd. She wanted a break from the dining hall food."

Debbie climbed out of the car. The dining hall food was pretty good, although their pizza didn't compare with the Buona Vita's.

Paulette waved at Jaxon. "How are you doing?"

Jaxon climbed out of the back seat and gave his grandmother a hug. "Okay."

"Just okay?"

"A little tired."

Paulette placed the pizza in her car. "I need to get going so Sally's pizza isn't ice cold, but I've been thinking about something. Jaxon," she said, "was there a ball of yarn and a scarf in one of the boxes when we went through? Did I miss it?"

Jaxon shook his head.

"Did you see a ball of yarn and scarf in the storage shed?"

He shook his head again then smiled. "Was Grandpa a knitter without you knowing it?"

Paulette laughed. "I don't think so, but you know, he was a bit of a…collector." Paulette held up her hand. "I didn't call him a hoarder."

Debbie thought of her old English teacher. She'd recently found out the woman had been something of a hoarder too.

Jaxon smiled again. Then he said, "There wasn't any yarn in the boxes we went through. Dad showed us that ugly scarf. I have no idea where it came from."

"Me neither," Paulette said. To Debbie, she added, "I'll let you know tomorrow if Sally has any additional information for us." Paulette reached to open her car door. "Oh." She turned back to Debbie. "Did you talk to Katherine?"

"No. I left her a message but haven't heard from her."

"I think she's still in Uhrichsville."

"Do you have the cousin's number?"

Paulette shook her head. "I'll ask Sally for it."

"Sounds good. See you tomorrow." As Paulette climbed into her car, Debbie motioned to the boys. "Come on inside with me in case there's anything more you want to order."

Julian bounced forward but Jaxon said, "I'll just wait in the car."

"It's going to be cold."

He shrugged. "I'll be fine."

Debbie turned, disappointed that Jaxon seemed to be regressing in their relationship. He'd been fine last Saturday evening. But she knew she couldn't take it personally. He was a teenager, and perhaps he'd simply had a bad day.

CHAPTER SIX

*T*hat evening, as Debbie helped Greg clean up the kitchen, she mentioned what Paulette had said about his father, EJ, being a collector. "What did he collect?" she asked.

"Some things he was purposeful about." Greg held up a mug with *Gettysburg* written across it and the profile of Abraham Lincoln. "This was his. He collected mugs from places he visited." Greg put the mug in the dishwasher. "He also collected baseball hats. And sports memorabilia." He grinned. "And rock 'n' roll albums from the sixties and seventies."

Debbie's eyebrows lifted. "But not yarn?"

Greg laughed. "Not that I know of. Nor antique wedding rings."

A half hour later, as she drove home, Debbie thought about EJ. He was Vivian's middle child. He had three older siblings and three younger half siblings. EJ's father, Earl, was killed fighting in North Africa soon after EJ was born and had never seen him in person. So soon after, that if Vivian had sent Earl a letter announcing EJ's birth and a photo, Debbie doubted it reached him in time.

EJ could have taken the knitting project and ring from his mother's drawer, but there was no evidence that he had.

When Debbie arrived home, she started a load of laundry and then sat down with a cup of tea to watch her favorite mystery on public television. Afterward, she intended to work more on Vivian's story, but a series of yawns sent her up to bed instead.

The next morning when Debbie arrived at the café, Janet greeted her cheerfully. "I found some information on Vivian's parents, Richard and Charlotte Olson. Would you like to sit for a minute? I have everything ready to open. Coffee's already made. Want some?"

"Yes, please." Debbie had walked to work and had also underestimated how cold it was. Even though she'd bundled up, the wind had chilled her.

Janet poured coffee for both of them as Debbie hung up her coat and then put on her apron and work shoes.

"I already turned up the heat," Janet said. "Should I turn it up more?"

"Let's wait and see how warm it feels in an hour." Debbie hated to think of what their heating bill might be, but it was a cost of doing business in Ohio in the winter.

Janet handed Debbie a cup, and they both headed to the corner table. Debbie asked, "What did you find out? Greg told me a while ago he doesn't know much about the Olsons, so I know he'll be interested in anything you've discovered."

"Richard Olson worked for the railroad in England from 1915 to 1927. He and Charlotte married in 1916 and lived in London in the flat that had belonged to her first husband, Luc Dumont, who passed away in 1914 after an auto accident. He was from a wealthy French family and they had one daughter, Daisy."

Debbie nodded. "There are letters from Daisy among Vivian's papers. Greg knew nothing about her."

"It seems after the Olsons came to the US, Daisy inherited the flat in London from her father. By then she was married to Noel Chapman."

"He died during the war in 1942."

"Yes," Janet said. "Daisy was a volunteer ambulance driver for a time before that."

"She mentioned that in a letter too, but then what?" Debbie asked. "Did Daisy survive the war?"

"I honestly don't know," Janet said. "I couldn't find any information about her death. No obituary. No nothing. The Chapman family manor in Berkshire ended up going to a nephew of Noel's. That's all I could find."

When Paulette came in two hours later, she handed Debbie a slip of paper. "Sally wrote the address of the cousin in Uhrichsville where Katherine has been staying and her phone number. I think it's a landline. Marjorie Anderson is her name. She's another cousin on Ted's side of the family. Her grandfather moved to Uhrichsville before Ted moved to Dennison."

Debbie stowed the paper in her apron pocket. "Thank you. I'll call. If I don't get through to her, I'll stop by after work."

After Paulette left for the day, just after one, Debbie stepped into the kitchen and called Katherine's number. This time she couldn't leave a message—Katherine's voice mail was full. She called Marjorie's number and left a message.

Just before four o'clock, Debbie parked in front of Marjorie's. There were no cars in the driveway, but she climbed the stairs anyway to the large Victorian house with gingerbread trim. The snow, including on the roof, gave it a fairy-tale look. There was a heart-shaped wreath to the left of the front door. Debbie rang the bell and waited. She rang it a second time. Finally, she retreated to her car, deciding to text Sally to see if it would be all right if she stopped by Good Shepherd. Maybe Sally could give her more information to track Katherine down.

Sally replied immediately. I'M JUST FINISHING DINNER. I'LL WAIT IN THE LOBBY FOR YOU.

Debbie texted back. BE THERE IN A FEW MINUTES. She wondered if Sally had family photos in her apartment. If so, she'd like to see them.

Ten minutes later, Debbie sat in the lobby with Sally, saying, "I've called Katherine a couple of times. I tried again today, and her voice mail is full. I left a message for Marjorie Anderson. I even drove out to her house, but no one answered the door."

"Katherine drives a small SUV. Was it in the driveway?"

Debbie shook her head.

"Marjorie is at least twenty years younger than Katherine. She's on the go a lot—she volunteers at the grade school close to her, delivers for Meals on Wheels, and is also a member of a garden club, although she's not doing any gardening now, of course." Sally laughed.

"I should have thought to leave a note for Katherine," Debbie said.

"I think I have Marjorie's cell phone number in my room—in my address book. I forgot about that when Paulette asked for her number and I tried looking it up on my phone. I must have not put it into my phone contacts." Sally stood. "Let's go down to my apartment."

Debbie walked beside Sally through the hall, which was decorated with hearts with photos of the residents on them. "Kim was wondering if you have any photographs of your mother knitting or photos of any of her projects."

Sally slowed her pace. "You know, I don't think I do." She paused a moment and then said, "I don't think I ever thought to take photos of Mama's knitting projects. There could be photos of someone wearing one of the sweaters she made—I don't think I have any, but there may be some in the photos EJ had."

When they reached Sally's room, she unlocked it and led the way inside. Beautiful antiques filled the living area. A secretary desk with a padded chair. A drop-leaf table and two chairs with needlepoint cushions. Vases and figurines were positioned on a barrister bookcase. The small sofa and recliner were new but complemented the antiques.

"Your home is lovely," Debbie said.

"Thank you. Most of the pieces were from Mama. She had excellent taste and a good eye for well-made furniture."

"With so many children, I imagine well-made furniture was a priority," Debbie said, and Sally chuckled.

Debbie scanned the room again, looking for photos. On an end table next to the sofa she spotted one of a younger Sally and Brant next to an older man. On the bookcase was a black-and-white photo of another group of people. Debbie moved closer to it.

"That's our whole family after the youngest was born, Brenda, who is in Mama's arms," Sally explained. "I was fourteen. EJ was ten."

Debbie leaned closer. "What a beautiful family. What year was the photo taken?"

"1952."

Vivian had seven children over a fourteen-year span, along with the death of her first husband and possibly the disappearance of her sister. But even if Daisy seemed to have vanished from online records, it didn't necessarily mean anything had happened to her, or that she and Vivian hadn't kept in touch by other means, like the telephone, which wouldn't have left a historical trail. Also, she hadn't finished reading the letters and diaries, which might provide more light.

"Your mother looks so happy," Debbie said.

"I think she was. She always wanted a big family." Sally stepped next to Debbie and focused on the photograph. "We all look happy. I think in the years after World War II, the adults were so relieved that the war was over and that they could get on with their lives that they focused on the good and hoped for the best. Of course as children, we knew nothing else." She sighed and said, "Not that I didn't miss Daddy. I didn't have a lot of memories of him, but as the eldest I had more than any of the other kids. I tried to hold on to those memories as best I could. I know a lot of soldiers didn't talk about the war once they returned home, but Ted did share memories about Daddy. I think that helped all of us hold on to him, to feel as if we knew and remembered him more than we actually did."

"Do you remember anything else from the day Ted arrived with the things from your father for your mother?"

"I do, even though I was only eight. It seemed so odd to have a strange man wearing a uniform who served with Daddy show up. At first I thought he was Daddy." She paused and then exhaled. "Our grandfather broke his leg that day…" She gave Debbie a sad smile. "And just before Ted came, a package arrived from England. It contained some belongings from Mama's sister, Daisy. Whenever anyone says bad things come in threes, I think of that day. Except Ted arriving wasn't a bad thing—it turned out to be the best thing for all of us."

"Could the knitting project have come in the box from Daisy?"

"No," Sally answered. "I specifically remember that Ted brought it."

That seemed like a lot for an eight-year-old to remember, but Debbie wasn't going to question Sally's memories. Perhaps Vivian had confirmed the memory when Sally was older. "What happened to Daisy?"

"I honestly don't know. I don't know if Mama ever knew for sure." Sally shrugged. "Things were so chaotic after the war, and there were so many people displaced. Mama thought if Daisy stayed in England that she must have died. But she always wondered if she went to France at some point during the war."

So Vivian and Daisy had definitely lost touch. "Could she have gone back to France? Were people able to travel back and forth like that?"

"Not really."

"Tell me what it was like around the time your mother passed away. Who cared for her?"

Sally's eyes fill with tears.

"I'm sorry," Debbie said.

"No, that's all right." Sally sighed. "It's been over thirty years, but the grief still catches me by surprise. Loss is like that. You would think I'd be over the loss of Mama, considering everything I went through with Dan…" Her voice trailed off. "Mama was only seventy-four, which is still a good long life. But now that I'm eighty-seven, I realize how young she was. And, of course, we weren't ready to lose her. Not that we weren't relieved to have her be out of pain."

She met Debbie's eyes. "EJ and I cared for her. Our five other siblings had all left town—our sisters came home now and then. They—Carol and Lottie and Brenda—all lived in Chicago at the time. But the two younger boys lived in Texas. Lottie, who had always been close to Katherine Johnston, came home for a few days right before Mama passed away, and the other two sisters came for the funeral. But, sadly, the younger boys didn't make it."

Sally took a deep breath. "There had been some back and forth over the ring between Lottie and me. It seemed it was worth something, and she thought we should sell it and split the money, but Mama had told me she wanted me to have it. However, I realized after Mama died, it was missing. Lottie assumed I'd taken it—but I can assure you I did not. I grilled her pretty hard, and I was convinced she hadn't taken it herself. Which left EJ. But he always denied it, and I didn't have any proof, so I gave up asking him."

"I see," Debbie said. "Are any of your other siblings still alive?"

"Only Lottie. She still lives in Chicago."

"Are she and Katherine still close?"

"Yes," Sally said. "As close as ever, I believe."

Sally stepped away from the photo and motioned Debbie toward the sofa. "I'll go get my address book."

As Sally walked down her little hall, Debbie sat down and turned her attention to the photo on the end table she'd noticed earlier. She guessed, by Sally's current appearance, that the photo was taken a few years ago. Sally stood in the middle and had a smile on her face. The older man with white hair next to her, Debbie assumed Sally's husband, had a hint of sadness in his eyes. He was thin and seemed weary. Brant stood on the other side of Sally and squinted into the camera.

"That was taken after Dan was diagnosed with lung cancer. We had four more years. The last year, however, was excruciating for him. Thankfully we were able to move in with Brant—I don't know what we would have done without him."

"I'm sorry," Debbie said.

Sally shrugged. "From Dan's first diagnosis to when he passed away was over thirty years, so we were lucky. But he was ill a good part of the time. Just when we thought he'd beat one cancer, it would show up somewhere else." She held up her address book and then recited a number.

Debbie put the number into her contacts. "What made you decide to leave Columbus and move back to Dennison?"

"I needed a fresh start." Sally chuckled. "Funny to call returning to my hometown a fresh start, but I was so sad after Dan passed I didn't want to stay in Columbus. Plus, Brant needs to get on with his life. He went through a divorce ten years ago, and he's been dating the sweetest gal for the last year. I hope they'll get married. I think they're more likely to with me not around." Sally chuckled. "Then again, depending on how long I live, I may not be able to afford to stay here at Good Shepherd. Brant may be stuck with me again in the near future."

Debbie shook her head. "I doubt Brant would feel stuck with you."

Sally shrugged. "Well, I hope that won't happen. But we'll see. If I get that ring that Mama intended for me in the first place, I may have to sell it to keep living here."

As Debbie drove home, she thought about what Sally had said. Wanting the ring for Brant could be a reason for Sally to stage the ring showing up. She couldn't give it to him without revealing she'd taken it all those years ago. If it suddenly showed up in Brant's possession, she would have to admit she'd taken it.

But that didn't make sense, if she truly was concerned about her personal finances. If she did have the ring and needed money, she wouldn't want to give it to Brant. She could simply have sold it somewhere, kept her finances secret, and pocketed the money. No one in the family would be any the wiser.

And Debbie wasn't any wiser about the mystery either.

That evening, Greg picked up Debbie to take her to dance class. When they arrived, Meg greeted them. "We are so enjoying having the two of you in our class. What made you decide to take it?"

"We needed a refresher before Valentine's Day," Debbie said. "We took classes before the dance last year and had so much fun, but haven't done much dancing since."

"The dance last year was wonderful," Meg said. "That's what got us back into teaching again."

"What got you into swing dancing in the first place?" Debbie asked.

"I had a neighbor years ago who loved music from the 1940s. She used to play her old records. Glenn Miller. Ella Fitzgerald. Bennie Goodman. All the greats. I loved to listen to the music when I visited. Or when she had her windows open in the summer."

More students arrived, and Meg floated off to greet them. Debbie sat beside Greg to change into her dancing shoes. Jeff started off the music with the Lindy Hop, and Greg stood and extended his hand to Debbie. She took his hand, stood, and let him lead her out to the floor. They practiced several triple steps, and then Meg welcomed everyone and instructed them to gather around her and Jeff.

As they practiced, Debbie realized she felt more relaxed and she and Greg were moving in unity—until she stepped on his foot again.

"Don't worry about it," he said. "Just keep going."

She tried to, but then she stepped on his foot a second time.

This time he laughed, and she did too.

After class, they exited into the cold. The streetlights lit up the winter wonderland, as did the bright half-moon and shimmering stars. "What a beautiful night," Debbie said.

Greg smiled at her. "It would be a good night for a drive."

"You know," she said, "I've been wondering where your grandparents' farm was. Could we drive by there?"

He clicked the fob to his truck. "Sure." He opened Debbie's door. "The view of the moon will be even better up at Grandma's place than here."

She grinned. "Prove it."

Fifteen minutes later, they were on a county highway going over a rolling hill east of Dennison and Debbie had caught Greg up on everything she knew about Daisy. "There it is." Greg pointed to the right and then pulled over on the left side of the road where they had a view of an old white farmhouse with black shutters and trim. Off to the left was a red barn. "The place looks good," Greg said.

"Who owns it now?"

"Neighbors bought it and rented it out after Grandma passed away," Greg said. "I'm not sure who owns it now."

"How many acres is the farm?"

"Forty or so. Enough to graze cattle and grow several fields of crops."

"It's a lovely property. At least from what I can see." Debbie gave Greg a wry smile. "The moon isn't actually visible right now."

Greg laughed. "That's entirely the fault of the clouds." He craned his neck to look out the windshield of his truck just as his phone beeped. He took it from his jacket pocket. "Julian," he said. "He needs help with his math assignment." He sighed.

"Duty calls," Debbie said.

"I'm sorry."

"Don't be," she answered. "Julian and his algebra are important. That doesn't mean I'm not. I understand."

As he pulled the pickup around and started back down the highway, a vehicle came toward them. In the passenger-side mirror Debbie saw it turn into the driveway past the farm. It appeared to be a large pickup.

"Sunday would be Grandpa's one hundred and eighth birthday," Greg said. "Dad always said a special prayer of thanks for his father on his birthday."

"Would you like to do something to commemorate it?" Debbie asked.

"Maybe," Greg said. "I'll talk with Mom and Sally and see what they think."

They were silent the rest of the way into town. When they reached her house, Greg jumped out of the pickup and hurried around to open her door. Then he walked her up to her porch and gave her a quick kiss. "I'll call in the morning," he said.

"Talk to you then. Good night." Debbie turned to her front door and unlocked it. It was getting close to bedtime, but Vivian's story was calling to her.

CHAPTER SEVEN

Connor Farm, Dennison, Ohio
March 4, 1942

*Vivian opened the front door and stood still for a
moment. Sally was singing "This Little Light of Mine,"
and Carol was babbling. Then a soft voice said, "Girls,
let's tidy up before your mama comes home. Sally, you
put the puzzle away. Then we'll have our snack."*

Earl's mother, Mary Connor.

*Vivian stepped into the living room and then
around the corner into the dining room.*

*"Mama!" Sally called out and slipped down from
her chair. "Grandma Mary is here." Carol held out her
arms to Vivian.*

*"Will came over to help Earl with the chores, and I
decided to come with him. I knew it was your knitting
circle day." Mary squinted. "Vivian, are you all right?"*

Vivian tried to speak, but her voice caught.

"What's wrong?" Mary asked.

Vivian sent Sally into the kitchen for a bib for Carol and then said, "I had a letter from my sister. Her husband was killed in the Battle of Singapore."

"Oh dear." Mary put her arm around Vivian and squeezed her shoulder. Carol began to fuss, and Vivian picked her up, holding the baby tight.

Sally ran into the dining room with the bib, and Mary went into the kitchen. She returned with a plate of freshly baked biscuits and the butter dish. "I made a stew for dinner," Mary said. "And a double batch of biscuits. Let's have one now. I have a pot of tea steeping."

Vivian turned to her mother-in-law. "Thank you." Holding the baby with one arm, she put her other hand to her chest. "You're so kind."

Mary and Will stayed for dinner and didn't leave until the dishes were done and the girls were in bed. After they were gone, Earl put on Gene Austin's "Now You're in My Arms" on the record player and turned the volume on low. Then he took Vivian's hand and led her to the couch. "Tell me what's wrong," he said.

She told him about Daisy's letter and about Noel being killed. He put his arm around her. "We'll pray for Daisy," he said. "And for peace. Please write to her and send our condolences. She can come here to live with us if she wants."

"I will." What Vivian couldn't say was how fearful she was. Would Earl be drafted? Would he be sent to the Pacific? Or across the Atlantic to Europe? Would he be killed too?

Earl let go of Vivian, stood, and took her hand and pulled her up. Gene Austin sang, "...and now you're in my arms..." Earl drew Vivian close—as close as possible considering she was eight and a half months pregnant—and began leading her across the living room floor as he sang along.

He twirled her around as the music stopped. When she faced him again, he said, "I know you're worried about me and about our little family, but fretting won't change anything. We need to go on living our life—and loving each other. We have to trust God with our future."

He was right.

"Keep up with the children, the house, and your knitting. I'll keep farming and caring for you and the girls. We, along with the rest of the world, will get through this war one way or another." He pulled her close again. "What matters is now and that we have each other."

Vivian tossed and turned that night, thinking about Daisy. Her sister had been twenty when she'd married Noel. Vivian had been enchanted with her older sister, her beau, and all the events around the wedding.

The ceremony took place in Daisy's paternal grand-parents' Normandy chateau. Daisy wore a gown from a Parisian house—satin with a V-neckline, long skirts with layered flounces, a train, and sheer long sleeves with daisies embroidered along the hems.

Vivian was the only attendant and wore a knee-length dress, also with sheer sleeves and embroidered daisies. The Dumont family had brought it from Paris too, along with a pair of glossy white shoes with silver buckles, a lace shawl, and a small white purse. Vivian had never worn such a fancy outfit.

Daisy's father, Luc Dumont, had grown up in Paris but spent summers in the chateau. In 1904 his father sent him to London to open a new branch of the family textile business. A couple of years later he married Charlotte Smith, Daisy and Vivian's mother, who worked as a secretary in his firm. Luc passed away when Daisy was seven. Charlotte married Richard Olson, Vivian's father, a few years later.

Daisy was Vivian's whole world, along with the flat and the Hyde Park neighborhood, which was all Vivian knew. Her father traveled with his work for the UK Railway, which was in the process of being nationalized. Mummy was often quiet and distant, but Daisy was warm and loving. Vivian always dreaded summer when Daisy would go to France to stay with her Dumont family for six weeks.

Vivian had mixed emotions the day of the wedding. It was an exciting time with the lovely clothes, the wedding events, the out-of-town guests, and the romance between Daisy and Noel, who was as handsome as Daisy was beautiful. But Daisy would now be spending part of her time in Berkshire at the Chapmans' country estate.

And that wasn't all. Vivian would be moving in a few months to the United States with her parents. Her father had been hired by the Pennsylvania Railroad as an inspector. Daisy would completely take over the London flat, which had been left to her by her father.

"You'll come visit me," Daisy had said. "When you're older, you can come without Mummy. We'll go to the theatre together in the evenings. We can take my children—when I have some—to the park during the day. And I'll visit you in the US too."

Vivian fell asleep rehearsing the memories. She didn't dream—or didn't remember her dreams—and she woke up in the morning still filled with grief. That afternoon, as the girls napped, she wrote Daisy a letter.

Vivian had never returned to England once she left, and Daisy had never visited the United States. Nor had she had children. Vivian mourned the handsome Noel and all her sister had lost—but she also mourned the time they'd lost between them. She brushed away a tear. Daisy had been so nurturing. She would have made a wonderful mother. Life was nothing but unpredictable, with both the tragic and the joyful.

Her heart ached as she finished the letter with All my love, your sister, Vivian.

The next day, Vivian hurried out to the coop to tend to the chickens while Earl was still in the house with Sally and Carol. On her way back inside with the basket of eggs, the baby kicked several times, and then a contraction gripped her. She gasped.

Perhaps the baby would come sooner than its due date, which was still a couple of weeks away. Before she reached the house, she stopped and leaned against the fence.

Earl called out from the back door. "Everything all right?"

Vivian waved. "I think so."

Earl came toward her, his hand outstretched. Another contraction. A few moments later, her water broke. Earl helped her into the house and called his parents.

A half hour later, Earl drove as fast as he could to town, to Twin City Hospital on First Street. The next morning, Vivian held the new baby, another girl, in her arms in her hospital room. She was small but healthy.

There was a knock on the door. "Come in," she said, hoping it was her mother. Earl had called the afternoon before to give them the good news. It was her father.

"Daddy," she said.

He stepped to the side of the hospital bed. "Congratulations." He leaned down to give her a kiss. "Your mother isn't feeling well, but she sends her love."

Vivian tightened her arms around her baby. "What's wrong with Mum?"

"The same," her father said. "She's feeling extra nervous today."

"I know she's worried about Daisy," Vivian said.

"Daisy has resources," Daddy said. "She'll be fine."

Vivian hoped so.

"What did you name the baby?"

"Lottie," Vivian answered. "Well, Charlotte, after Mum. But we'll call her Lottie."

Dad smiled. "I think that will thrill your mother."

"Will you tell her, please?"

"Yes."

Once she was home from the hospital, her mother-in-law helped Vivian every day with the girls, the house, and the garden. When Vivian had regained her strength, she drove Lottie into town to meet her other grandmother. Dad was off inspecting the railways and the woman who kept house for them was working, making dinner and tidying up.

Mum smiled at the sight of little Lottie but refused to hold her. "I might drop her."

"No," Vivian answered, "you won't. You were a good mother to Daisy and to me. You took good care of us."

"I need you to hold her," Mum said. "I'll sit beside you." She did, patting Lottie's little feet as they visited.

The next week, Vivian took Lottie to the knitting circle, where the women passed her around and cooed over her. The weeks flew by. Some days, Vivian didn't worry at all about Earl being drafted. It seemed perhaps life would go on with the war far away and Earl safe at home. But then on a rainy night in the middle of

March, after the girls were all asleep, Earl put an album on the phonograph but turned the volume down low.

Vivian already had her nightgown and robe on, but Earl took her in his arms. Instead of dancing, he held her. "I received my draft papers today," he said. "I report in May."

CHAPTER EIGHT

Thursday morning, as Debbie served waffles, two orders of omelets, bacon and eggs, and a giant cinnamon roll to a party of five, her phone buzzed in her apron pocket. She made a mental note to check it when she had a chance.

Harry, Crosby, and Patricia came in fifteen minutes later. Debbie quickly served Harry a black cup of coffee and started Patricia's peppermint mocha. When she delivered it, Patricia said she'd heard that Greg had a mysterious ring in his possession.

Debbie put a hand on her hip and cocked her head. "Where did you hear that?"

"From Sally Watts," Patricia said. "She's an old friend of Pop Pop's."

"Is that so?" Even though she'd grown up in the town, Debbie couldn't get over all the connections between people in Dennison. There was so much she hadn't seen—or noticed—when she was young.

Patricia said, "It seems to be a reverse whodunit. Instead of searching for a thief, you're looking for the opposite." Patricia paused for a moment then said, "Even if you were trying to figure out if it was stolen around the time Vivian passed away, the theft would be way beyond the statute of limitations now."

"I'm sure you're right about that," Debbie said. Patricia had the distinction of not only being Harry's beloved granddaughter but also one of Dennison's busiest attorneys. "We're operating under the assumption that a family member most likely had the ring for the last thirty-plus years. Greg would like to know who put it in the box that landed on his porch and why, and who the ring should belong to now."

"Sounds like quite the puzzle," Patricia said.

"Did it come from the Connor family?" Harry asked.

"I don't know," Debbie answered. "Sally thinks it came from Earl Senior, from when he was in the war. She remembers Ted Johnston bringing it with him the first time he came to the farm."

"Hmm," Harry said. "That has me thinking about Vivian Connor."

"Do you remember her?"

"Yes." His face brightened. "I was just a boy the first time I saw her. She was sitting in that old truck of Earl's, a Ford. Maybe a 1929 or '30 model. Earl bought it while still in high school back when lots of people couldn't buy a vehicle. He was working as a farmhand for various people and hauling people and things in his truck, making money any way he could. And then along comes Vivian for their senior year, and in no time they were a couple, a very handsome couple."

Debbie smiled at the thought.

"I remember Vivian's parents too. Mr. and Mrs. Olson." Harry lifted his mug to his lips.

"Richard and Charlotte."

He nodded, took a drink, then put his mug back on the table. "I knew him better than I knew her. Mrs. Olson kept to herself. Mr. Olson though, he was an inspector for the railroad. He was a friendly man. I saw quite a bit of him through the years."

"When did you become friends with Sally?"

"She worked at the depot when she was in high school. Her grandfather got her the job in the ticket booth. She was a responsible gal, probably from being the oldest in a big family."

"Did she work after school?"

"Yep," Harry said. "And on Saturdays."

"How did she get back and forth to the farm?"

"She lived with her grandparents once she was in high school."

"Oh." That surprised Debbie. She wondered why Sally had never mentioned it. "Didn't Vivian need her help at home?"

"Probably, but Sally was a good student and involved in school activities besides working part-time. She would have had to take the bus home right after school to the farm if she didn't stay in town. Ted and Vivian both had chores to do in the late afternoon. They couldn't be driving in to get her."

Harry leaned back in his chair. "About the time Sally graduated high school, her grandmother died, and then her grandfather was transferred to Pittsburgh."

"Oh. That's too bad."

"Richard managed to stay in Dennison far longer than most railroad men—I think it was so Charlotte could be close to Vivian and her family. But I think Richard was a wanderer at heart and ready to move on. I'm guessing he came back to see Vivian and the kids often enough though."

That information made Debbie want to talk with Sally again and find out more about her family, although she doubted it would help solve who ended up with—and who returned—the ring.

Business slowed by ten o'clock, and Debbie checked her phone while in the kitchen. She didn't recognize the number, but whoever had called had left a message. She listened to it—Katherine Johnston. "I heard you've been trying to track me down. I'm back in Chicago but plan to return to Uhrichsville on Saturday. Could we meet then? You can either come to my cousin's house or suggest another place to meet. Call me at this number—my cell phone—when you have a chance."

Debbie quickly returned the call, but it went straight to voicemail. After leaving a message, she slipped her phone into her apron pocket. Why would Katherine go home to Chicago, only to return to Uhrichsville so soon?

After Debbie cleaned the café and prepped for the next day, she went straight home to get ready for Julian's middle school basketball game in Holmes County. He was riding the bus with his team, and she, Greg, and Jaxon were all going to watch. Julian would ride home after the game with all of them.

Debbie quickly changed into jeans and a Claymont High School sweatshirt. Then she pulled on her boots. Downstairs, she made a pot of decaf, and while it brewed she made a hot chocolate for Jaxon and poured it into a travel mug. Then she poured coffee into two more travel mugs for the trip. Once she had all the mugs in a bag, she put on her warmest parka, grabbed a knit cap and her insulated gloves, and stepped to the front door just as Greg stopped outside. She grabbed her purse and the bag and opened the door.

Greg left the motor running and jumped to the street from his pickup as she started down the steps.

"I have coffee for us and a hot chocolate for Jaxon," Debbie called out.

"Great! Mom's with us—but I already grabbed a coffee for the road. So it's all good."

Debbie was surprised but pleased that Paulette was attending. She didn't usually go to out-of-town games.

Greg opened the truck's front door for Debbie.

"I'll sit in the back," Debbie said.

Greg shook his head. "Mom and Jaxon are all settled."

Before she fastened her seat belt, Debbie turned and said hello and passed the drinks. Paulette thanked her. Jaxon said something unintelligible. She guessed it was some expression of gratitude.

It was a half-hour drive to Hiland High School. At first everyone in the pickup was quiet, but then Paulette asked Jaxon about his project for his US history class. As Greg pulled off I-77 onto Highway 39, Jaxon said he'd been researching the Battle of El Guettar in Tunisia in March of 1943, growing more animated as he talked. Clearly, the subject was interesting to him. "My great-grandfather Earl was there," he said. "It was the first time the Allies were able to defeat the German tank units. Nobody really won the battle. But it did lead up to the Allies invading Sicily."

He paused, and Debbie heard a slurp from the back seat. He must have taken a sip of cocoa.

"Sounds like you're doing a great job on your research," Debbie said.

"Well, it's interesting," he admitted. "But the coolest stuff I found out is about code-breaking. The Allies could decipher German messages, and it made a big difference in North Africa. There weren't as many spies in North Africa as other places. And the Allies eventually won."

"What are some examples of the other places?" Greg asked.

"France and Italy mainly. They also had spies in Germany— German-Americans who could speak the language. And some German POWs being held in France. And German women."

"That's fascinating," Debbie said.

"Spies discovered stuff like troop deployments and where the staging areas were. That helped the Allies plan their advances," Jaxon explained. "Because they didn't have many spies in North Africa, they had to rely more on intercepting and decoding German intelligence."

They were on the outskirts of Sugarcreek, which was Amish country, and passed an Amish restaurant.

"Are your classmates as knowledgeable about World War II as you are?" Paulette asked.

Jaxon answered, "I'm not that knowledgeable, but I'm learning a lot."

"I'd say you are." Paulette sounded proud of her grandson, and she had reason to be. Debbie was impressed too.

"Maybe it's all those World War II movies Dad watched with us, and knowing my great-grandfather died fighting to defeat the Nazis." Jaxon was silent for a long moment and then said, "Debbie, have you found anything in those boxes?"

She turned a little in her seat so she could see him. "Yes. Not anything about your great-grandfather war experiences yet, but lots about what it was like for the family before he left for the war and quite a bit about his parents and his wife's parents and sister."

"Oh." He sounded disappointed.

Debbie wanted to encourage him to stay interested in the topic. She said, "Your great-grandmother Vivian had a sister who was half French."

"I didn't know that. Was she in France during the war?"

"I don't think so," Debbie said. "But she was in London during the Blitz. She had a flat—an apartment—near Hyde Park that was demolished by a German bomb."

"Wow!" Jaxon sounded a little too enthusiastic, but Debbie knew it was the connection to the war that intrigued him, which was a welcome surprise. Julian was interested in history, but Jaxon usually wasn't. "On an even sadder note, her husband was in the British Navy and was killed in the Battle of Singapore."

Paulette leaned backward. "That's not a battle we hear much about, is it?"

Debbie agreed. "It was a few months after Pearl Harbor. We'd just entered the war. Vivian was heartbroken for her sister and started wondering if Earl would be called up."

"Speaking of Vivian," Paulette said, "I've been thinking about her boxes more. Julian said they were taped when he saw them Saturday morning. Jaxon, were they still taped when you carried them into the house that afternoon?"

"One was," he said after a short pause. "But the other was like someone tried to tape it back down but it popped up. I figured you had added something to the box after I left on Friday after school."

"No," Paulette said. "I didn't. They were both taped—completely—when I dropped the boxes off."

"The one with the yarn and scarf wasn't taped when we arrived," Greg said. "I think we can safely say someone opened one of the boxes while they were on the back porch before Jaxon carried them inside."

The four sat a few rows above the Claymont team bench. Julian started the game as a forward but picked up three fouls in the first quarter, and his coach benched him at the beginning of the second quarter. He glanced back at Greg who gave him a thumbs-up and a smile. Debbie appreciated how encouraging Greg was with his sons. She was sure it was a key component of his close relationship with them.

"He's playing too rough." Jaxon's voice was loud, and Julian turned his head again. "Lighten up," Jaxon said to him. Julian quickly directed his attention back to the game.

"Julian knows what to do," Greg said. "He'll figure it out."

Jaxon stood. "I'm going to go sit at the top of the bleachers."

The game was tied at halftime. Julian started again for the third quarter. He didn't foul again until the middle of the fourth quarter when the score was tied again. Jaxon groaned so loudly that Debbie could hear him.

Paulette grabbed Debbie's hand and quietly said, "I don't know whether to be upset about Julian having four fouls or how loud Jaxon is being."

Greg leaned across Debbie and said to his mom, "Neither are worth getting upset about, believe me. Although it seems it's time for me to have another talk with Jaxon about showing Julian some grace."

The coach didn't pull Julian out of the game. Debbie thought about siblings. Both she and Greg were only children. Jaxon was a bit overbearing as an oldest child, but he and Julian were only two years apart. She thought of Daisy and Vivian's ten-year age difference. Daisy seemed so loving and caring with Vivian from what Debbie had read, but that was probably to be expected with such a large age gap.

Julian shot a three-point basket and broke the tie. Jaxon whooped from the top of the bleachers. Greg high-fived Paulette and then Debbie, letting his hand linger on hers as he grinned.

Hiland immediately scored two points.

With thirty seconds left and the Mustangs up by only one point, the center on the team fouled Julian. Greg called out, "You've got this!" as Julian stepped to the line. He missed the first free throw but made the second one.

"Don't foul!" Jaxon yelled as Julian started down the court, reaching for the ball. The Hiland player quickly dribbled the ball and took a shot. He missed, but Hiland got the rebound. Another shot went up. This time Julian got the rebound.

Julian chest-passed the ball to a teammate, who passed it to the center, who put up a shot. But he missed too. Julian grabbed the rebound. For a second Debbie thought he'd shoot, but instead he passed it back to the team's center, who took a shot and made it. As Hiland passed the ball, the buzzer rang.

Greg stood and started clapping. Debbie and Paulette stood too.

A half hour later, Julian came out of the locker room. As they stepped into the breezeway of the gym and walked to the parking lot, Jaxon put his arm around Julian. Debbie expected Jaxon to compliment Julian on the game.

She was right. "Good—I mean, great game," he said. "It was your best yet."

Julian stepped to the side and playfully punched Jaxon's shoulder. "Thanks."

Paulette's hand flew to her chest. Greg reached for Debbie's hand. "Maybe they'll be all right after all," he whispered.

"I think they *are* all right, now," Debbie whispered back. There were many times Debbie wished she had a sibling—and now was one of those.

Jaxon put his arm around Julian again and drew him close. "Not to take the focus off you." He laughed. "We were talking about the boxes on the porch on the way to the game. Were they taped shut when you carried them into the house?"

"No," Julian answered. "Well, one was. But the other was open."

"Are you sure?"

"Positive," Julian said. "I tried to re-tape it but it popped back open. Why?"

"Just wondering."

Julian put his arm around Jaxon and they continued walking, matching their steps and strides.

How could Vivian stand to go for so long without seeing Daisy? How could Daisy stand not seeing her little sister? Granted, people in the 1940s weren't able to travel like today, especially not during a war when the Nazis torpedoed Allied ships in the Atlantic and shot down planes in the sky.

Debbie both looked forward to and dreaded finding out the rest of the story. She knew it didn't have a happy ending with regard to Earl or Daisy's husband. But she still didn't know Daisy's story. What happened to her?

CHAPTER NINE

F riday late morning, Debbie's parents came into the café. She hurried around the corner and gave each of them a hug.

"How are you feeling?" she asked.

"Good," Mom replied, her voice a little hoarse. "We're running errands."

"I need more salt for the walkways," Dad said. "I let my supply get a little low."

That wasn't like him. "Would you like your usual? Two black coffees?"

"I'll take an herbal tea," Mom said. "I'm cutting back on caffeine."

"I'll take my usual." Dad motioned toward the pastry and dessert tray. "And we'll take two of whatever is Janet's most delicious recent creation."

Debbie laughed. "That's going to be hard for me to choose for you, but I'll do my best." She decided on the mini vanilla pound cake and a piece of raspberry cheesecake. Debbie delivered them along with the tea and coffee. "Mom, I'm so glad you're feeling better. It's only a week until the Valentine's Day dance."

Mom glanced at Dad and then back at Debbie. "We'll see about going."

"Why wouldn't you?" She searched her mother's face. She did look a bit wan.

"I'm not feeling up to par yet."

"I thought you just had a cold."

"It *was* just a cold. I guess I'm not bouncing back as quickly as I used to."

"You need to get a lot of rest in the next week. I'll bring soup over tonight."

Mom smiled. "Dad made a batch of chicken noodle soup yesterday. We'll have leftovers tonight."

A group of four people came through the door. Debbie gave her parents a wave and then welcomed the customers, motioning to the open table in the back. As she grabbed four menus, she feared she hadn't taken her mom being ill seriously enough. Her parents were getting older. Was she in denial about that?

The day kept getting busier and busier. Mom and Dad left, and a lunch rushed ensued. After it ended, Janet left for the day and so did Paulette. Soon after, Eileen pushed Ray's wheelchair into the café. Debbie craned her neck to see who was holding the door for them. Sally.

"Hello!" Debbie called out. "Welcome!" She met them and took the chair from Eileen, pushing it to the closest table. "What brings the three of you in?"

"We've been reminiscing." Eileen swung her purse off her shoulder and hung it on the back of the chair. "And we thought the depot would be a good place to spend some time this afternoon. An aide dropped us off."

Debbie pushed Ray up to the edge of the table and Sally joined them, sitting across from Eileen.

"Would you all like coffee?" Debbie asked.

Ray and Eileen nodded as Sally said, "Black tea for me."

"How about a valentine goodie? Janet has been baking up a storm. My treat."

Eileen rubbed her hands together. "What a nice surprise."

Debbie returned with the coffees and a plate of truffles, cheesecake bars, and chocolate hand pies. After she refilled the coffee mugs of the customers at the back table, she poured herself a cup of coffee and stepped to Ray, Eileen, and Sally's table. "Mind if I join you for a few minutes?"

"Please do," Ray said. "We were talking about who all used to live in the railroad district. All three of us did at one time." Ray grinned. "And now you do."

Debbie smiled in return. "Did all three of you live there at the same time?"

"Yes." Sally picked up a truffle. "I lived with my grandparents during high school. Eileen was down the street, and Ray was a few blocks away." She took a bite.

"Harry Franklin mentioned that you lived with your grandparents," Debbie said.

Sally finished the truffle. "Their house has been renovated since Grannie and Grandpa Olson had it. The house was bumped both up and out. I wish we would have had that much room—for a year Carol and Lottie lived there too."

Debbie leaned back against her chair. "What was that like?"

"I loved living in town, but I did miss the farm. Especially Mama and the little kids. We'd go home on the weekends though, usually on Friday night after the football game or basketball game or whatever was going on. Mama didn't want us to miss out on the school activities—she'd always felt a little on the outside, having lived in England until she was ten and coming here. She didn't want us to feel like that." Sally took a sip of coffee. "But I also think she thought it would be good for Grannie to have us around. She tended to be moody, but when we were there she rallied. She had help—a woman who came in to do the cleaning and laundry and make dinner, but Grannie would make us breakfast and make sure our clothes were in good order and go over our homework. It gave her a purpose." Sally's expression softened. "She was a special lady."

"Did she knit?"

Sally shook her head. "Not that I know of. I never saw her knit."

"Did your mother keep knitting after the war?"

"Yes. She didn't sit down much for years, or if she did, she had a child in her lap." Sally laughed. "But then after she was older, she got back into it. If I hadn't first seen that project when Ted brought it to the farm that day, I might think it was from when Mama taught—or tried to teach—one of my sisters to knit."

"Did you learn?"

Sally laughed. "Mama tried to teach me, but I was horrible at it. I managed to learn how to crochet some, but I never mastered knitting. I think Lottie was the only one of us who could do it."

"Do you think she would remember the scarf and ball of yarn?"

"Sure," Sally said. "Lottie was pretty curious. I remember one time when she got into Mama's bottom drawer and saw the scarf and found the ring. Mama scolded her."

"Do you remember the knitting circle from church that your mother used to go to?"

"Of course," Sally answered. "The knitting circle continued after the war."

That surprised Debbie. "Really?"

"They knitted items for missionaries after that, along with making quilts. Mama was part of that group again in the early seventies or so. But it petered out over the years till it finally disbanded."

"That was sad," Eileen said. "The knitting circle did so much good—for so long."

"There's a new, young group of knitters at the church," Debbie interjected. "I wonder if they'll add some charity projects once they learn the basics. 'Knit your bit,'" she said, repeating the wartime motto. Daisy had done so much for the war effort. She liked to think that Daisy had time to indulge her gift for knitting too. Perhaps she too had knit items for the British soldiers being sent off to war.

Debbie had already decided to go over to the museum after the café closed to show Kim the yarn and scarf. She'd put the project in a bag that morning and brought it to the café but had opted not to mention to Ray, Eileen, and Sally that she had it with her. It probably wouldn't be a good idea to bring it out into public until they knew more. On the other hand, maybe she should have. Perhaps the sight of it might have flushed out the culprit who'd put it in the box on Greg's porch. But there was no sense in speculating now.

She grabbed the bag and hurried through the lobby to the museum. As she neared the front doors, Kim came out wearing her coat and carrying her purse. "Are you leaving?" Debbie asked.

"Barry has a lab appointment. I should be back in about an hour."

"How is he doing?"

"About the same. The doctor wanted to do some more bloodwork."

"I know you have a lot going on, but could you stop by the café when you return?" She held up the bag. "I brought the knitting project."

"Sure." Kim waved and started toward the parking lot.

Debbie headed to the café, put the bag with the knitting project on the first table, and then began cleaning the dining room. She finished her closing duties and prepped for the next day, but Kim still didn't return. She hoped nothing was wrong.

Debbie had just put on her coat and was about to retrieve the knitting project when a knock sounded on the front door. She unlocked and opened it.

Without saying hello, Kim said, "Sorry I'm late. Barry was feeling lightheaded after the blood draw, so I got him a snack at home."

"Is he all right?" Debbie asked.

"I think so. He sometimes gets queasy. I think that's all." Kim smiled. "I'm anxious to see the scarf."

Debbie moved to where she had set the bag and took out the ball of yarn and scarf. She put them both on the table.

Kim sat down and examined them. "Do you think it's from a wartime project?"

Debbie shook her head. "According to what Vivian wrote in her diary, the yarn for items made for soldiers was a drab olive green. For sailors, it was navy blue." She tilted her head. "What color is this? Taupe?"

"I don't think it's dyed at all," Kim said. "Natural wool, I'd guess. It's so rustic—it's definitely hand spun."

"Goodness," Debbie said. "Was most yarn back then hand spun?"

"No, but there were people still spinning wool on those old spindles. There still are." Kim pointed to the knitting needles. "I've never seen anything like these."

"They're rather rustic too, aren't they?" Debbie leaned closer. "I thought maybe that's what all knitting needles looked like in the 1940s."

"I don't think so." Kim sat up straight. "Did you try asking Bonnie at Sticks & Threads in Uhrichsville?"

"I called earlier when I had a break. The shop is closed for a few days while Bonnie is on vacation."

Kim nodded. "Well, I know of another knitting shop in Akron. KnitOhio. The owner's first name is Liana. I think she might be able to help you. Take the yarn, needles, and scarf with you. See what she says."

As Debbie walked home, she looked up the knitting store and called to see if Liana was working that day. The woman who answered put her on hold. After a few minutes, another woman said, "Hello, this Liana. How may I help you?"

"Kim Smith from the Dennison Depot Museum recommended that I contact you," Debbie said.

"I remember Kim," the woman said. "I stopped by her museum a year ago or so, and we had a wonderful conversation."

Debbie explained about the knitting project and what she was hoping to learn. "Kim thought you might be able to identify the yarn and the approximate age. The needles too. I thought I'd drive to Akron now, if you'll be in the shop until closing."

"I will," Liana answered. "And I'd be happy to take a look at what you have."

"Perfect. I should be there shortly." Debbie ended the call. Jaxon had a game in West Lafayette, but Greg had a business meeting in Canton and was going to go straight to the game. Julian was getting a ride with a friend. Debbie might as well drive to Akron. She hurried home and grabbed her keys. As she headed north on I-77, more snow began to fall. She went straight to the knitting store and found a place to park around the corner from it.

The shop was in the first story of an old house. Inside, the yarn was organized by type and color, making for a kaleidoscope of hues. The cash register was on a counter between the two rooms.

An older woman with short gray hair and large brown eyes welcomed her. The name tag on her sweater read LIANA.

"Hi, Liana. I'm Debbie Albright. I spoke with you on the phone."

Liana's eyes lit up. "That was fast. Show me what you have."

Debbie put her bag on the counter. "Someone put this in a box of things from my boyfriend's grandmother, but no one knows who put it there. However, an elderly aunt remembers the project from when she was growing up."

Liana reached for the knitting needle first but then stopped. "Is it all right if I touch it?"

"Yes," Debbie said.

Liana ran her index finger along the length of the wood. "These are made out of oak. I'd say they're from the early 1900s and most likely from Europe by the look of the knobs."

Next, she rubbed the yarn and then ran it through her fingers. "It was hand spun, that's for sure. And old."

"How old?"

"Not as old as the knitting needles. I'd guess 1930s or '40s. It's likely not anything that was produced around here."

"How can you tell?"

"Well, I've never seen anything similar, and I've handled a lot of fibers in my day. I have a couple of contacts, experts I've met at knitting conferences. Do you mind if I text them photos of the yarn and scarf and see if they might know anything?"

"That would be great. Thank you. Vivian, who passed away in the early 1990s and owned this at one time, was born in England and lived there until she was ten."

"So it might have come from England?"

"Maybe. But her daughter thinks a friend brought it with him after World War II. She has the idea, and has since she was a child, that her father, who died fighting in North Africa in 1943, gave it to the friend just before he died. Then the friend brought it to her mother, Vivian."

Liana cocked her head and smiled. "That's quite a story."

Debbie laughed. "I know."

Liana said, "I have a knitting friend who lives in Scotland. I'll text her. If we can identify the wool and therefore the sheep, we could have an idea of where the yarn originated."

"That would be great—but what about the odd pattern, if you can even call it a pattern? It seems so random. Any ideas about that?"

Liana picked up the scarf. "I assumed it was some sort of sampler."

"I've heard of a cross-stitch sampler before but not a knitting sampler."

"They were more common years ago. I remember doing one as a girl, when I first learned to knit. They're a way to practice different stitches." She turned to the shelf behind the counter and retrieved a pair of glasses. Holding them up, she laughed. "Maybe these will help." She put them on and then picked up the scarf, or sampler, or whatever it was. "Interesting." She ran her finger over one of the stitches that stuck out at an odd angle. "I've never seen anything like this," she said. "Sure, it could be a sampler. If so, it's not a very good one. Or maybe it's just someone's attempt to make a scarf and to practice purling and knitting. Maybe someone who was forced to learn to knit who really didn't want to."

Debbie looked more closely at the scarf. Again, all she saw was a mix of bumps and vees, but no distinguishable pattern.

Liana took out her phone again and snapped a few photos of the scarf. "Do you mind if I share these with my contacts too?"

"Not at all," Debbie answered. "I appreciate anything you can do to help solve the mystery of where this came from and what it is." Debbie took out her business card from her purse. "This has my cell phone number on it. Text or call and let me know what you find out."

Liana slipped her phone in her pocket and took the card from Debbie. "I'll text my contacts ASAP. I love a good mystery."

After Debbie said her thanks and put the project in the bag, she headed home to Dennison. She'd make a quick sandwich and spend the rest of the evening going through Vivian's boxes.

CHAPTER TEN

Vivian felt numb as she cared for the two older girls, nursed Lottie, and tended the house and garden. Earl went about his work, but added tasks. He chopped more wood and stacked the pile high. He trimmed the trees around the house. He fixed several shingles on the roof. He replaced a board on the barn and then painted the whole thing.

His parents came to the house for several hours each day to help. Vivian mostly sat and rocked the baby, who was colicky, while Mary cooked, cleaned, and tended to Sally and Carol.

Everyone seemed to know what to do except for Vivian. Sometimes she followed Earl around, usually carrying the baby, and asked him about what she needed to know. When did he order the feed for the chickens? How much? When should she breed the cows? When should she wean the calf? How many female piglets should she keep from the next litter? What was the vet's phone number?

Vivian had wanted four babies by the time she was twenty-four. But as she walked Lottie up and down the porch every evening, she wondered how she'd be able to care for three children by herself. She breathed a prayer of thanks for her in-laws. What would she do without them? Her father's job was so demanding he hardly had any time to help. Mum certainly wasn't up to helping much.

Even with help, Vivian wasn't sure how she'd care for the children, get the chores done, keep up with the farmwork, and do the books for the business too. Earl assured her his dad would see to the actual farming, but he was aging. She wasn't sure that he could do it all, and the farm didn't make enough money for her to hire anyone. Plus, there wasn't anyone available to hire, even if she could afford it. All the men were being drafted. She tried not to worry, but she wasn't successful.

She also had a nagging worry about Daisy. Was she truly all right? Where would she live now that Noel was gone? The Chapman family estate in Berkshire would most likely go to Noel's sister's son, who was in his late twenties. It wouldn't go to Daisy. Vivian would write Daisy again and ask her.

Vivian finally received replies to her last two letters from Daisy at the end of April.

Fortunately, the nephew was allowing Daisy to stay in Berkshire for the time being as he was working for the war department in London, and his wife and child had gone to Edinburgh to live with her parents.

I don't expect I'll stay here long though. Please don't be alarmed if you don't receive letters from me regularly. I'm going to do my best to be as helpful as I can to put an end to this dreadful war. I may not be able to write. Please don't worry.

Vivian definitely wouldn't tell Mum that. Vivian couldn't help but worry more about Daisy than before. Between fretting about her sister and dreading Earl's upcoming departure, Vivian realized she didn't have much milk for the baby. Mary insisted she drink peppermint tea and rest, but even after following her advice, Vivian's supply didn't improve. In fact, it dwindled even more.

Lottie became fussier. Vivian went to the doctor, who recommended she feed the baby evaporated milk. By the next week, Vivian had lost her milk altogether.

Earl went for his Army physical a few days later. His health was good and there was no indication he wouldn't pass, but Vivian wished he wouldn't. Perhaps his feet were flat. She'd heard of men not passing a physical because of a skin rash or poor eyesight.

It was her last and only chance to not lose her husband to the draft.

She sat on the porch, giving Lottie her bottle while Sally and Carol played with their dolls late in the afternoon. Mary cooked dinner inside, and Will was in the barn, milking the cow. The days were growing warmer, and she soaked in the afternoon sun.

She heard the truck before she saw it. Earl turned up the driveway. He honked and waved and then tipped his fedora. Her heart hurt at the sight of him. She took the bottle from Lottie's mouth, put the baby to her shoulder to burp her, and stood.

Sally called out, "Daddy!" and ran. Carol toddled after her. Vivian caught Carol's hand and, balancing Lottie, helped Carol down the stairs. At the bottom, Carol took off running toward where Earl had parked the truck. He jumped to the ground, took two steps, and then swept both Sally and Carol into his arms. Both squealed in delight. Vivian's heart began to press against her chest again.

How would they survive without Earl's hugs and joy and playfulness? He looked over the heads of the girls and gave Vivian a smile.

"I take it you passed," she said.

He gave her a nod. "I'm in perfect health. As I should be."

She wasn't surprised. She knew he would make a fine soldier.

"I report to Akron next week."

Her knees grew weak, but she focused on the baby in her arms and steadied herself. Life had felt so easy from the day she met Earl, the first day of their senior year. Now it was about to get very, very hard. She had to be strong.

Mary and Will came to the farm to tell Earl goodbye the day he left for basic training. Vivian stood back and watched as they hugged their son.

Both were stoic and matter-of-fact. Earl, in his pressed uniform, looked confident and movie-star handsome. After he hugged his mother and shook hands with his father, he picked up Sally, tossing her in the air and making her laugh. Then he hugged her. Next he picked up Carol and hugged her too.

"You girls help your mama, okay?"

Sally nodded, and Carol copied her.

"Come, girls," Mary said, taking Lottie from Vivian. "Let's put the baby down for her nap, and then you can help me in the kitchen. Let's start a batch of cookies."

Sally ran ahead, and Carol followed. Earl picked up his suitcase and opened the truck door for Vivian. He swung his suitcase into the bed of the pickup, and Vivian climbed into the passenger side.

Will stood at the end of the driveway and waved as they drove away.

As they neared the train station, Earl found parking on the street two blocks away.

"I'll walk you in to the depot," Vivian said.

"If you don't mind," Earl answered.

"Of course not." She planned to go to her knitting circle that afternoon, and it still didn't start for another hour. She had time—and she wanted to spend every last minute with Earl that she could.

Earl grabbed his suitcase. "Write to me with any questions you have that Dad can't answer," he said. "I might not be able to answer for a few weeks, but I will as soon as I can." She knew he'd be back for a short homecoming. But then he would ship out. Probably to England, she guessed. Maybe he'd even find Daisy *there, a thing she knew was almost impossible, but she could hope. She had to have hope, about so very many things.*

As they entered the depot lobby, someone called out, "Vivian! Earl!"

She turned. Daddy jogged to meet them. He wore a long coat and had a briefcase in one hand. "Are you leaving today?"

Daddy extended his hand to Earl as he reached them. "I'm glad to see you before you leave." Then he turned to Vivian. "How are you, darling?"

"Holding up."

"Good, good." He shifted his briefcase. "Well, Godspeed, Earl. I hope we'll see you again before you ship out."

"I should be back the beginning of August. I have three months of basic training."

"Good. We'll see you then." Daddy tipped his hat and said, "And we'll see you very soon, Vivian."

And then off he went toward the platform, walking briskly and swinging his briefcase.

Vivian sat down on a bench near the aid station as Earl stepped to the ticket booth. A few minutes later, he sat beside Vivian. Several soldiers stopped at the aid station for doughnuts and coffee. A woman, just a few years younger than Vivian, served them. She wore bright red lipstick and had her hair styled in a roll at the back of her neck. She smiled and laughed.

Earl reached for Vivian's hand, squeezed it, and held it. "I'm sorry to be leaving you, for so many reasons."

"I know." Vivian leaned her head against his shoulder. "But we'll be all right." She exhaled and said, "And what you'll be doing is important. Necessary. This war has to be turned around. Remember that while you're in basic training. And later. And I'll remember that every day that you're gone."

He let go of her hand and put his arm around her, pulling her close. A train whistle blew. Vivian pressed her face against his shoulder.

The girl at the canteen laughed.

Vivian, at twenty-three, felt years beyond her age.

Earl kissed the top of Vivian's head and then stood. So did she. He wrapped his arms around her and pulled her close. The whistle blew again.

Earl glanced to the platform.

"You need to go." Vivian took a step backward.

She needed to let him go.

Later that afternoon and during the next couple of months of knitting circles, Vivian knitted as fast as she

could—gloves, sweaters, socks, scarves. She prayed for the men who would wear the items, and for Earl too.

The last Wednesday of July, Will stepped into the church fellowship hall, his hat in his hand. Alarmed, Vivian stood. Had something happened to Sally or Carol? They had been making bread with Mary when Vivian left the farm.

Will saw her and waved.

She put down the scarf she was knitting and started toward him. "Is everything all right?"

"Yes." He smiled. "Earl called. He's coming in on the three o'clock train. He has a three-day pass before heading east. I wanted to let you know so you could stay in town and pick him up."

Vivian's knees felt weak. She'd only had one letter from him in the last three months. But now he was coming home. "Thank you," she said.

Vivian returned to the scarf she was making for Earl—she wanted to send it with him. When Daisy first taught her how to knit, she'd told Vivian about a woman in Belgium who knitted code into various projects about the trains passing by her house and then delivered the information to a spy. Several days ago, Vivian had wondered out loud during dinner about knitting a message into the scarf for Earl. Will answered, "You could knit Morse code in it—Earl

*knew it before being inducted. He knows it even bet-
ter now."*

"Oh," she said. "What a good idea. Do you know it?"

*"I do, from my railroad work. What would you like
to code into his scarf?"*

"I love you."

*Will smiled and grabbed a pencil and a piece of
paper from the desk. After he finished, he handed the
paper to Vivian. She stared at the dots and dashes.
She would purl one for the dots and knit three for the
dashes. She'd need to knit quite a few stitches between
the words. Seven would do. She'd started to work on it
that evening, planning to work the code in near the end
of the scarf. Although she'd used the same olive green
yarn, knitting Earl's scarf was much more meaningful
than what she'd knitted before for other soldiers. She
hoped it would bring him comfort.*

*Vivian left the knitting circle a few minutes early
and headed straight for the station, skipping her usual
stop to visit with her mother for a half hour or so. Three
days. That meant on Friday, just after noon, he would
board the train east for—she had no idea where.*

*But for now, he was home. Vivian counted every
moment. He put on his work clothes and mucked out
the barn and stacked the latest cutting of hay. He cut*

more firewood for winter. He sat beside Vivian in the evening, holding her hand.

At times he seemed too quiet, too far away. Vivian watched him and gave him space. Other times he seemed engaged, playing with the girls, teasing his mother, talking seriously with his dad.

All of them wanted to be by his side as much as possible. Thursday evening after they'd put the girls to bed, Vivian gave him the scarf. She pointed out the code. He ran his fingers over it and then laughed.

"I love you too."

Then he put a few albums on the record player. The last song was "Now You're in My Arms." He pulled Vivian out of the rocking chair. As the music played, he began to lead her. A rock step. A triple step to the right. A triple step to the left.

"I can't bear to think about how much I'm going to miss you," he said.

Vivian put her head on his shoulder.

"It's going to be harder than I expected." He stroked her head. "Being away was much worse than I thought it would be, but I need to press on. I'll do my part—and give it my very best. I'll miss you and our family every minute I'm gone."

"And we'll miss you."

He pulled her closer as Gene Austin crooned. He bent down and kissed her forehead. And then her mouth. She kissed him back, both hands around his neck now as they danced, long past the time the song ended.

She would remember this night as long as she lived.

CHAPTER ELEVEN

*D*ebbie read Vivian's entry for July 31, 1942.

> *Mary and Will, the girls, and I all took Earl to Mum and*
> *Daddy's this morning so they could tell him goodbye. Mum said*
> *something to him in private—I have no idea what it was. She*
> *assumed he was headed to England. But he's not. He'll ship out*
> *of Norfolk, Virginia, to North Africa as part of the 2nd Armored*
> *Division. I doubt he'll need the scarf packed in his rucksack,*
> *though I've heard the nights can be cold in the desert.*
>
> *After we told Mum and Daddy goodbye, Earl drove us—*
> *all crammed in the pickup—to the depot to tell him goodbye.*
> *We walked him into the lobby and hugged him and told him*
> *farewell. He looked so handsome in his uniform. I had such*
> *a mixture of emotions. Pride and fear and sadness all mixed*
> *together. Sally cried, and Will picked her up and swung her*
> *onto his shoulders. Mary carried Carol in her arms, and I*
> *had Lottie in mine. When we reached the pickup, I heard*
> *Earl call my name. We all turned, and there he was at the*
> *very end of the platform, waving at us. "All my love, until*
> *we meet again," he called out. I blew him a kiss, and he blew*
> *one back. Sally waved from atop her grandfather's shoulders.*

*The whistle blew, sending steam into the summer sky, and
the conductor called out, "All aboard!" Earl turned, his profile toward me for just a second. Then he was gone. I've been
brave for the girls but feel numb inside, as if I've lost a part
of myself.*

Debbie read the passage a second time. Her heart ached for this
family.

Blinking back tears, she shifted to the stack of photos, this time
looking for any knitted items. There was a photo of the children in
the snow with the date *1948* written on the bottom. Several of them
had mittens on and scarves wrapped around their necks. Another
showed an unidentified little girl, who was probably five or so, wearing a cardigan sweater. Debbie placed both photos aside.

She kept going through the photos, stopping when she came to
a group of soldiers standing next to a tank. She gasped. Earl had his
sleeves pushed to his elbows but wore a scarf around his neck. He
held up his hands, seemingly to show off the gloves without fingers
that he wore. The other soldiers wore the same kind of gloves too.
Debbie squinted at the photo. That was most likely the scarf Vivian
had knitted *I love you* into.

Could the mysterious scarf's odd pattern be Morse code too?

She took it out of the bag. It had purled stitches of one and three
combinations. She studied each of the men. Was that a young Ted
standing next to Earl? Having seen photos of Ted at Greg's house, she
was certain it was. She flipped the photo over. On the back someone
had written *Outside of Casablanca, December 1942.*

Before Debbie went to bed, she boxed up art supplies for the valentine-making activity at the depot the next day. As she finished, her phone dinged with a text from Greg. JAXON'S TEAM WON! I SPOKE WITH BOTH MOM AND SALLY. THEY BOTH THINK IT'S A GOOD IDEA TO MEET UP AT THE OLD FARM ON SUNDAY TO MARK GRANDPA'S BIRTHDAY. THEY WOULD LOVE FOR YOU TO GO WITH US. WHAT DO YOU THINK?

Debbie texted back. TELL JAXON GREAT JOB ON THE GAME! SOUNDS GOOD AS FAR AS GOING UP TO THE FARM. I'D LIKE THAT.

She was tempted to ask if the current owners of the farm would mind, but she guessed they wouldn't. Besides, Sally or Paulette— or both—most likely knew the current owners and would ask for permission.

The next morning, Debbie walked into the depot to find Janet and Ian setting up a table for the crafting that would start at ten. "Good morning!" she called out.

"Good morning to you!" Ian called back with his hint of Scottish accent. He passed Debbie, heading toward the front. "Sorry to have to rush away."

Debbie gave him a wave.

"How are you?" Janet asked.

"I'd say I'm cold, but I think it's become my normal state." Debbie put her box of supplies on the floor by the first table. "Where are the tablecloths?"

Janet pointed to a box by the café door.

As the two worked, Debbie told Janet about the plan to acknowledge Earl Connor Sr.'s birthday on Sunday.

"What a great idea!" she said. "I think it's wonderful that the Connor family is still engaged in their history enough to do that."

"I do too." Debbie unfurled a tablecloth. "Having Paulette give the boxes of Vivian's things to Greg right now is really timely."

Janet pulled on the other end, covering the table. "Any word on the ring?"

"No." Debbie told Janet about meeting Liana the evening before. "I hope we'll hear back from her soon about the yarn."

Janet lifted another tablecloth from the box. "Have you found anything more about Vivian's sister?"

"No."

"I told Ian about Daisy disappearing," Janet said. "He said his grandmother told him some people completely vanished during the war. She went from Glasgow to London to work as a nanny before the war started and then ended up staying. She lived in Chelsea. A bomb destroyed a building a few blocks away. Nothing was left. Perhaps Vivian's sister was in another building when it was bombed, and her body was never identified."

"Could be." Debbie winced. "And we know sometimes people disappeared on purpose during the war. Maybe they weren't hit by a bomb—maybe they reinvented themselves or moved somewhere completely new and went by a different name."

Janet nodded. "Do you think Vivian's sister might have done that?"

"I have no idea." Debbie shrugged. "It's probably just wishful thinking, considering the alternative."

Starting at nine forty-five, Paulette and Janet worked in the café while Debbie finished setting up the valentine-making supplies— construction paper, doilies, old cards, lace, sequins, and stickers. Templates for hearts and cupids. Glue and scissors. Hole punches and stamps.

Kim came through the depot a few minutes before ten, bundled in a parka, gloves, and boots. She pressed one hand to her chest. "I forgot about this."

"Today's the day," Debbie said. "How is Barry doing?"

"Better. We haven't gotten all the test results, but we're hopeful he's on the mend." She pointed to the museum. "I'll be back after I get out of this coat."

Debbie placed a heart template on a piece of red construction paper and then traced around it. As she began cutting it out, an older woman and a little girl came through the front door. "Is this where we make valentines?" the woman asked.

"Yes," Debbie said. "Choose from the supplies on the tables."

"Stickers!" The little girl appeared to be five or so.

"How much does it cost?" the woman asked.

"It's free." Debbie motioned to the café. "But we'd love it if you'd make at least two, one to take home and one to display at the dance on Friday evening."

"Wonderful." The woman smiled. "Thank you."

More people stopped by over the next half hour, and then senior citizens from Good Shepherd began to come in, including Sally, Eileen, and Ray.

"How nice of you to come," Debbie said as she went forward to meet them. "Especially when it's still so cold."

"Good Shepherd is sending another van after this one," Eileen said. "We managed to get in the first one."

"Because Sally ran ahead and saved our spots." Ray winked. "We want to make sure to get back in time for lunch."

Debbie laughed. "Well, if you're on a deadline, you'd better get started." She motioned toward the tables. "Sally, I have a few photos to show you if you don't mind."

"Of course not."

Debbie hurried into the café. Business had slowed some, and Paulette was wiping down tables. "I'm just grabbing a few photos to show Sally," Debbie said. "Come out when you have a chance. She's here with Eileen and Ray."

Paulette said, "I will. But Janet is coming out first. She has some treats to share."

"Perfect." Debbie stepped into the kitchen, grabbed the envelopes from the drawer where they kept their purses, and gave Janet a wave. "See you soon!"

Janet held up a plate of frosted cupcakes. "Strawberry." She licked her lips. "I'll be right out."

Debbie stepped back into the lobby to find a couple and their two boys. They'd already found a table and were looking through the supplies. Debbie stepped to Sally's side. "Kim asked me to look for pictures of your mom's that had knitted items in them. I found these." She pulled the photos out of the envelope, showing her the one of the group of kids wearing scarves and mittens.

"That's me, Carol, Lottie, and EJ," Sally said. "It was probably taken around 1949. Bobby, Ted's first son, would have been a baby, not quite one year old."

"How about this one?" Debbie showed her the photo of the little girl wearing the sweater.

"That's Lottie." Sally laughed. "No wonder she took up knitting. What a cute sweater."

Next Debbie showed her the photo of Earl with the other soldiers.

"I don't remember this picture." Sally took the photo from Debbie. "It's Daddy." She squinted. "And that's Ted." She held the photo closer to her face. "Look at that scarf Daddy's wearing even though it looks like it's hot out."

"I noticed that," Debbie said.

Sally squinted again. "Do you think Mama knitted the scarf?"

"Yes. She wrote in her diary about finishing a scarf for him before he left. Any chance Ted brought it home?"

"Not that I know of." Sally kept staring at the photo. "It's comforting to think that he probably had the scarf on when he was killed, had something near him from Mama."

"She wrote in her diary that she knitted 'I love you' into the scarf in Morse code."

Sally patted her hand against her chest. "I had no idea." She handed the photo back to Debbie.

"I'll ask Kim to have the photo enlarged. Perhaps we'll be able to know for certain if it's the same scarf."

Sally's eyes grew misty. "Thank you. That means a lot."

As Debbie tucked the photos back into the envelope, Janet came out with the cupcakes. Debbie turned toward the museum. She might as well show Kim the photos now. But as she started across the lobby, Kim stepped out of the museum.

Debbie held up the envelope. "I found two photos with items that Vivian knitted and a possible third. Sally just identified the people in the pictures." Debbie took the photos from the envelope and showed her the first two with the children.

As she showed her the image of Earl Sr. with Ted, Kim beamed. "This is perfect for the exhibit."

"I agree," Debbie responded. "There's a chance Vivian knitted Earl's scarf. She wrote about completing a scarf for him the night before he left."

"We'll never know," Kim said.

Debbie answered, "We might." She explained about Vivian coding *I love you* into the last few rows of the scarf. "Do you think you could have the photo enlarged and see if you can make out the details of the last rows?" Debbie slipped all three photos back into the envelope.

"I'll get it to our photographer this afternoon." Kim motioned to the envelope. "Hold on to that until after I make a valentine for Barry. He deserves one more than ever this year."

After the valentine-making event finished at one o'clock, Debbie cleaned the tables and then carried the box of tablecloths to her car to launder later at home. As she made a second trip with the box of art supplies, a woman with her white hair piled on her head and her hood down approached. "Any chance you're Debbie Albright?"

"I am," Debbie answered.

The woman swept her hand across her forehead in a dramatic gesture of relief. "I'm Katherine Johnston. I heard you're looking for me."

Debbie wished she didn't have a box in her hand and could mirror back the same gesture. Instead, she said, "I'm so pleased to meet you! Do you have a few minutes? I just need to put this in my car."

"Yes," Katherine said.

"Would you like to go into the café and find a table? Paulette's inside. I'll be right in."

The woman took a step closer to the door. "Sure."

A few minutes later, Debbie joined Katherine and Paulette. Each had a cup of coffee, and a plate of Janet's heart-shaped shortbread drizzled with milk chocolate lay in the middle of the table.

Debbie sat down next to Katherine. "Did Paulette tell you what we found in the box of EJ's things?"

"Yes," Katherine said. "But I heard it first from Lottie, who heard about it from Sally. So the ring really did turn up after all."

"It did. Why were you so sure it was still around?"

"Just a hunch." Katherine picked up a piece of shortbread. "That ring intrigued me for years. When I was about twelve, my father took me to Dennison to visit Uncle Ted, Aunt Vivian, and their seven children. Lottie—who must have been sixteen or so—first showed me the ring, rather covertly. It was in her mother's bottom bureau drawer stuck in a ball of yarn. It was the weirdest thing. Lottie said it was worth a lot of money—which as an adult I realized I needed to take with a grain of salt. She also said her mother would never talk about it."

Debbie smiled, hoping to encourage Katherine to keep talking more.

She did. "Last month, I found out that the Johnston family was once wealthy. Quite wealthy. But they lost their money, except for one valuable ring, during the stock market crash in 1929. I put two and two together and came up with Vivian's ring. So I talked to Lottie, who didn't know who ended up with it. I left messages for Sally, but she didn't return them. So I decided to drive down and see what I could figure out."

Up till now, they'd been operating under the assumption that Sally was right and the ring was a Connor heirloom, not a Johnston one. But Katherine's story was plausible. "You really think Vivian's ring came from the Johnston family?" Debbie asked.

"Yes, absolutely. Once I learned the family used to be wealthy, I went through all of my father's letters. There's one from my grandmother to my father mentioning a valuable ring in the family that would someday be his. I'm positive Vivian's ring originated in the Johnston family."

Paulette coughed and then said, "I've never heard anyone else say that."

"Don't you think it's common sense? Grandmother Johnston had a valuable ring that mysteriously disappeared. Vivian had a mysterious and valuable ring that no one knows the origin of that also mysteriously disappeared before turning up again. I've wondered about the ring nearly all my life. I'd like to finally find out what happened to it—and not just how Greg has it now, which in itself seems suspicious."

Paulette crossed her arms. "Are you insinuating my husband took the ring and hid it from everyone—including me—all these years? Because I can assure you he did not."

Katherine shrugged. "I'm not saying he did. But why did it turn up in a box left by you on Greg's porch?" She glanced from Paulette to Debbie.

Debbie cleared her throat and said, "Katherine, is it all right if I ask you a question?"

"Of course."

"Where were you last Saturday?"

She laughed. "What is this, some kind of detective show? You're turning this around on me? You think I've had the ring all these years and decided to plant it in one of EJ's boxes that landed on Greg's porch? Why would I possibly do that?"

Good question. "All I asked is where you were last Saturday."

"Fine. I was snowed in at my cousin Marjorie's house. On Monday, she had the driveway plowed. On Wednesday, I drove to Chicago because I had a get-together with a group of retired friends that I hang out with once a month. And I returned here today because both Marjorie and Lottie said you wanted to talk. Call either one, they'll vouch for me."

"Thank you," Debbie said evenly. "That's good information to have."

"And now I'm going to come right out and say it. Ted stole that ring, and then someone from the Connor family ended up with it." Katherine stood. "When you find out who, let me know. Then give it to me. My grandmother intended that it go to my father, the oldest in the family. Instead, Ted stole it, from his own mother and brother. I want it back. If my father inherited the ring as intended, it would be mine now."

Debbie tried to put the conversation with Katherine out of her mind as she practiced her steps during dance class, but she couldn't help but be distracted.

Greg seemed distracted too. "Sorry," he said.

"What for?" Debbie asked.

He grimaced. "Stepping on your foot."

Debbie stared up at him. "You didn't."

"I did."

Chuckling, she said, "I didn't notice."

Greg smiled. "What are you thinking about?"

She whispered, "The ring. Who did it belong to? Where has it been for the last thirty years? And how did it end up on your porch?"

"I take it you're no closer to cracking the case?"

"That's correct. I'm more confused than ever." She glanced up into his face. "What's distracting *you*?"

Smiling again, he shrugged as Meg called them back to the center of the room. "Is everyone doing all right? You look a little like my sheep do when they turn around and get lost." She grinned. "Let's do a couple of exercises to loosen everyone up."

She led them in shoulder rolls and then shaking out their arms and hands. "We only have one more lesson after this one until the dance," Meg said. "Let's make tonight count. Everyone close your eyes and imagine dancing in the depot like it's 1945 and the war has finally ended."

What a wonderful image, Debbie thought. The rest of the class went a little better, now that her head was filled with something other than the mystery.

Greg dropped her off after class. As she unlocked the door to her house, her phone dinged. She expected it to be Janet or one of the very few people who would text her after nine. Once she was inside, she slipped off her gloves and pulled her phone from her pocket.

Liana. Finally!

I HEARD BACK FROM ONE OF MY CONTACTS WHO LIVES HERE IN OHIO. SHE DOESN'T THINK IT'S A SAMPLER—SHE SAID SHE'S NEVER SEEN ANYTHING LIKE IT. SHE CAN'T IDENTIFY THE WOOL EITHER BUT GUESSES IT'S PROBABLY FROM EUROPE. I TEXTED AN ACQUAINTANCE IN SCOTLAND TO SEE IF SHE CAN HELP. I HOPE I'LL HEAR BACK FROM HER SOON.

Debbie thanked Liana for the information. She hoped she'd hear back from her European contact soon too. In the meantime, Debbie had one other place to seek out more information—Vivian's boxes.

CHAPTER TWELVE

Dennison, Ohio
October 14, 1942

Vivian left the knitting circle early with a half-completed sleeveless sweater in her bag, destined for an unknown soldier. Perhaps after North Africa, Earl would be sent to Europe. He'd need warmer clothes then. She'd knit a sleeveless sweater and gloves next just in case.

The sun shone brightly, but a cold wind blew through the autumn day. Instead of heading home, Vivian drove to Dr. Roy's office for her appointment. She wanted her suspicions confirmed before writing to Earl.

She didn't have to wait long before Dr. Roy could see her. As she sat on the exam table, he asked about Earl. After giving him an update, Vivian said, "I'm expecting, but I'm hoping you can confirm it."

"Have you had morning sickness?"

"Some."

"Fatigue?"

She laughed. "I have a four-year-old, a two-year-old, and a baby. Plus a farm. I'm always tired."

"Do you have help?"

"Thankfully, yes, Earl's parents have been a god-send," she answered. "I welcome another baby. So will Earl." She was near exhaustion all the time, especially with this pregnancy. But still the thought of another baby thrilled her.

"We'll need a urine sample to send to the lab," Dr. Roy said. "But I'm guessing you know as well as the lab if there's a baby on the way."

She nodded. "I'm sure there is."

"Do you want to do the test anyway? It will take a week or so."

"I remember." She'd had a pregnancy test with Sally but not the other two.

The doctor's office called a week later, in the morning. The nurse said, "Mrs. Connor?"

"Yes," Vivian said.

"Your test is positive. According to Dr. Roy, your due date will be the twenty-first of April."

Tears sprang to Vivian's eyes. "Thank you."

She wrote to Earl that evening after the girls went to bed. She would wait to tell the girls, but the *next day she told her father- and mother-in-law. Both were happy to hear the news. She wished her own mother would react so positively, but that was never a given. She supposed she'd find out.*

That night as she stared at the ceiling, unable to sleep despite her eyes growing heavier by the minute, her happiness turned to fear. What if Mary or Will fell ill—or worse? She couldn't do this without them. What if Earl didn't come home? She chastised herself for thinking that way. Dark thoughts did no good.

She pressed her hand against her belly and breathed a prayer of thanks for the baby and then a plea for strength and sustenance. If the baby was a boy, she'd name him after Earl.

At the end of November, Vivian finally had a letter from Earl in response to her news. This baby is a gift from heaven, *he wrote. He said he had arrived, but the location had been blacked out along with a few other words and phrases in the letter. She knew an officer in Earl's unit read all the letters written by soldiers before they were sent. According to the news, she guessed he was in Morocco. That seemed to be where troops*

arriving in North Africa disembarked. Or perhaps he was in Algeria. Either way, Earl and the 2nd Armored Division were part of Operation Torch and were fighting against the Vichy French. According to news reports she'd heard on the radio, Germany would soon be sending more troops to North Africa.

I'm sorry I'm not home to care for you and our little ones. I pray this war will be over soon and that you'll be back in my arms.

She folded the letter and tucked it inside her Bible, determined to care for her family as best she could. She didn't want Earl to worry about her or the children while he was fighting the Nazis.

The first Friday of March, Vivian had an early morning doctor's appointment. She was six weeks from her due date. After hearing the baby's heartbeat and being assured that everything was fine, she drove Earl's Ford pickup to the railroad district to visit her mother, who—to her chagrin—she hadn't seen since Christmas.

When she pulled up to the house, the curtains were still drawn even though it was almost nine in the morning. She hadn't stopped by because she hadn't had the courage to tell her mother she was expecting again. She wasn't showing much at Christmas. But she couldn't put it off any longer.

Vivian knocked on the door. When no one answered, she opened it. The radio blared. Vivian called out, "Hello?"

She stepped into the house and entered the living room. Her mother sat in the dim light staring at the radio. "Have you heard from Daisy?" Her mother didn't even bother to greet her.

"No."

"There's been a horrible ordeal. An air-raid warning caused hundreds of Londoners to rush to the Bethnal Green Underground station. It was a crushing stampede. One hundred and seventy-three people were killed, including sixty-two children." Mum met Vivian's gaze. "Doesn't Daisy have a friend who lives near there?"

Daisy had a lot of friends. She could be anywhere.

"When was the last time you had a letter from her?"

Vivian swallowed. "Last June."

Mum's gaze shifted back to the radio. "That's when I last heard from her too. I'm afraid she's gone to France for some harebrained reason."

"By crossing the Channel in a small boat and landing on a beach?" Vivian shivered at the thought. If a wave didn't swamp the boat, a German patrol would have most likely gotten her.

Mum swiped at a tear. "I have a bad feeling about all of this. Call it a mother's intuition. I begged her to come to the US as soon as Noel was commissioned. If only she'd listened to me."

"England is her home."

"And France," Mum replied. "I told Earl if he ends up there to look for her. But now he's in North Africa, right?"

"Yes," Vivian said. "It seems the Allies will attack through Italy first instead of France."

"If they can get through North Africa," Mum said.

"They will." They had to. Vivian stood. "Have you had breakfast?"

Mum shook her head. "Mrs. Small had an appointment this morning."

"I'll make you an omelet."

"I don't want you waiting on me." Mum exhaled then stared at Vivian's swollen midsection. "Why didn't you tell me? How long until the baby is due?"

"The third week of April." There was no point in answering her mother's question about why she'd kept the news from her.

"I expect you're happy to have another, but I worry about your health." Mum wrapped her arms around her middle. "You have so much work to do without taking care of an infant again too."

"Please don't worry." Vivian stood to go into the kitchen. "As long as Earl is all right, I will be too." She still didn't know how she would manage with another baby, but she knew she had to. There was no other choice.

Later that afternoon, when the girls were down for a nap, Vivian went out to tend the chickens. She was surprised to see both her in-laws coming toward her. She hadn't expected them.

"We wanted to speak with you about something," said Will.

Vivian straightened and put her hands to her aching lower back. "Of course," she said.

"We don't want to intrude. Please make a decision that is best for you and the children." He paused. Then, "We'd like to move in with you," he said. "So we'll be here with you at night after the baby comes. Plus we'll be able to help more."

Vivian's heart constricted. "What about your place?"

"I'm already renting out the land. We'll rent the house too. That way when Earl returns, we'll be able to go back. I already have a man who works for the railroad interested. He wants a country place for his family. We would write up a lease for six months at a time." He smiled kindly. "You don't have to answer us now. Think about it."

"*I don't need to.*" *Vivian blinked several times as tears welled in her eyes. "It's unexpected—but greatly appreciated and an immense relief."*

Mary took her hand. "We'll start packing this evening."

Her in-laws moved in immediately. Two days later, she had a letter from Earl, her first in three months.

There are so many things I can't tell you, of course, one being of a very pleasant surprise that resulted in a gift for you. I'll tell you all about it when I come home. You won't need to remind me. Amazing to have some good happen among all the bad.

At the end of the letter he wrote, Please don't worry about me. I am surrounded by good men and competent soldiers who have become like brothers. Please pray for them too.

A gift for her? What could Earl possibly mean?

At supper that night, Vivian read the letter aloud, leaving out the line about the gift. Lottie began to cry, and Mary lifted her out of her high chair and patted her back as Vivian finished the letter. From articles in the newspaper about the 2ⁿᵈ Armored Division, she guessed he was in Algeria or perhaps even Tunisia by now.

Vivian had another letter from Earl two days later. He wrote that he was getting adequate food.

The aide station has caught up, and we are now able to shower once a week or so. It's warm during the day but cools down by night. Please take care of yourself—get enough rest and make sure you are eating enough. Please don't work too hard.

Vivian went into labor the next day, five weeks early, in the middle of the night. The contractions woke her, but she figured she had several hours before she needed to go to the hospital. But the contractions kept coming, closer and closer together. She knocked on her in-laws' bedroom door softly, not wanting to wake the children. Then louder. Finally, Mary opened the door. "Is it time?"

"Yes."

"We'll be right out."

Vivian changed into a dress and put on her shoes. Then she grabbed the bag she'd packed. Will met her in the living room, dressed and ready to go. Mary said, "The girls will be fine. Don't worry about a thing here."

Vivian wouldn't. She trusted her mother-in-law as much as she trusted herself with her children.

She had several contractions on the way into town. The sun rose behind them as they reached the hospital, and Vivian had another contraction as she climbed out of the pickup. By the time she waddled inside the front door of the hospital, she had the urge to push. The nurse at the desk walked her as quickly as Vivian could manage down the hall and into the delivery room. "I'll call Dr. Roy right now," she said. "Don't push."

Vivian changed into the hospital gown and leaned against the delivery table. The nurse raced back into the room. "Dr. Roy is on his way."

Another contraction. Once it ended, the nurse helped her climb onto the table. Dr. Roy breezed in a moment later and said, "Vivian, everything will be all right. Follow my directions."

Twenty minutes later, Earl Gregory Connor, Jr.— EJ—was in Vivian's arms. At just under five pounds, he was her tiniest baby so far, even smaller than Lottie. Had she worked too hard? Worried too much? Not eaten enough? Dr. Roy assured her EJ was fine, especially for being a month early. "He's healthy. What's important now is that you get your rest and the nutrition you need so your milk supply is ample. You'll need to feed him as often as he'll eat."

Will was EJ's first visitor at the nursery window. He was as proud as could be of his new grandson, but he told Vivian later the nurses only allowed him to stay for five minutes. He needed to get back to the farm to do the chores anyway and asked the nurse to tell Vivian, who'd been moved into a hospital room, that he'd be back that afternoon.

Vivian asked the nurse to call her mother with the news. She returned a few minutes later and said, "Your mother congratulated you."

That meant she wouldn't be coming to visit. What had Vivian expected? Her mother hadn't visited her in the hospital after the births of the girls either.

That evening, just before visiting hours ended, there was a knock on the door.

"Come in." Vivian tried not to get her hopes up.

The door opened, and her father poked his head into the room.

"Daddy."

He stepped forward, a pot of daffodils in his hand. "Darling," he said. "Congratulations. I just arrived and got the news." He put the flowers on her table. The bright yellow color of the forced blooms lifted her spirits a little. She decided she'd plant them near the house when she got home, so they'd return every year. If only Earl would return, she thought.

"I already stopped by the nursery and saw the little fellow," Daddy continued. "Not only does he have Earl's name, but he also looks like him."

"Do you think so?"

He nodded. "Your mother sends her love."

Vivian's face must have shown her disappointment.

"Don't be too hard on her. She's doing the best she can." He smiled a little. "She doesn't have your fortitude. In fact, I don't know where you got your strength. You've grown into such a strong young woman. I doubt there's a thing you can't do."

CHAPTER THIRTEEN

Connor Farm, Dennison, Ohio
March 30, 1943

Back at the farm with the new baby, Vivian cried herself to sleep. She wanted Earl home. Mary appeared exhausted too, and even Will seemed to be wearing down. The girls were out of sorts. Plus the garden needed to be prepared for planting, and the piglets sold.

They were barely getting the farming done, staying ahead of the upkeep of the house, and seeing to the children. She would have had to leave the farm if it wasn't for Earl's parents. But they were aging, and even with their help, she didn't know how much longer she could go on. Months perhaps, but not years.

"When will Daddy come home?" Sally asked the next morning at breakfast.

Vivian covered her mouth as she yawned then said, "When the war ends, he will come home." The last letter she'd had was dated a month ago. According to the newspaper, the 2nd Armored Division was now in Tunisia, fighting the Germans and Italians in the Battle of El Guettar.

After breakfast with the girls, Vivian fed the baby and put him in the bassinet. A cold front had blown in overnight and the temperature was below freezing again, so Vivian put on Earl's work coat and went out to feed the chickens and collect the eggs. Afterward she herded the cow into the barn.

When she returned to the house, the girls played by the woodstove, and EJ fussed in his cradle. The house smelled of coffee brewing and cinnamon rolls. Vivian would never stop thanking the Lord for her in-laws.

"You rest now," Mary said. "I'm afraid you're working too hard already. Go back to bed. You look exhausted. Remember what happened with Lottie?"

Vivian did. She'd lost her milk when Lottie was an infant. It wouldn't do any good for tiny EJ to be put on canned milk or cow's milk this soon. Lottie did all right, but often babies didn't tolerate other milks very well.

She did what Mary told her to, taking EJ into bed with her and burrowing under the quilts as if she were *a mama rabbit. She felt an overwhelming sense of sadness over Earl being so far away. And not knowing where Daisy was or if she was dead or alive. And barely having a relationship with her mother.*

At dinnertime, as she nursed EJ, Sally and Carol bickered over who got to use the one blue tin cup, as opposed to the others that were gray. Finally, Vivian snapped, "Give the blue cup to Lottie." Then she grimaced. She sounded like her mother. Just the thought took her back to her childhood when Daisy would read her a story and put her bed, "Because Mummy isn't feeling well." Sometimes Daisy would play one of her jazz records, but softly so Mummy couldn't hear. Sometimes she would make their porridge in the morning, "Because Mummy needs more rest." Yes, Vivian was exhausted, but was she also depressed? She didn't want her children to grow up with a mother who couldn't properly care for them. She'd had Daisy and Daddy. Her children had Will and Mary—but not forever.

Lord, *she silently prayed,* help me. Did she need more rest? Better food? Or had she inherited something from her mother that was making itself known now? She shuddered as she put the baby in the bassinet.

Sally handed her the blue cup. "We're sorry, Mama."

Vivian took the cup and wrapped her arm around Sally. Then she hugged Carol and then Lottie. "There's no need to fight over the blue cup. You can take turns or else I'll put it high in the cupboard until you're older. But I shouldn't have snapped at you. I'm extra tired lately, but it has nothing to do with the three of you."

The next day, Mary encouraged Vivian to go into town for her knitting circle. "You go by yourself," she said.

Vivian shook her head. "I shouldn't leave EJ this soon."

"Feed him before you go. He sleeps for three hours every afternoon. Leave the knitting circle a little early to come home. He'll be fine."

Vivian finally agreed. As she rounded the curve to town, shifting down to second gear, her heart lifted some. She'd been working on Earl's sleeveless sweater. All that was left was to add the binding on the neck. Her goal was to finish it soon and get it into the mail. He'd need it for when the Allies invaded Europe.

As she settled into her knitting, the rhythm and repetition soothing her as it so often did, Blanche sat down beside her. "Vivian," she said. "How are you?"

"All right."

"Busy with the new little one?"

"Yes. And the other three and the farm."

"You look tired."

Vivian smiled. "I have been," she answered. "But it's good to be here today. I don't have much left to do on this sweater."

"How is Earl?"

"All right," Vivian answered. She prayed that was true.

"I saw a newsreel last night at the theater. There was footage of the 2ⁿᵈ Armored Division."

"Really?"

"Yes, recent footage. In this new battle."

"The Battle of Guettar."

"Yes."

"What did they say?"

"That our soldiers are facing immense challenges but persevering."

That was what the newsreels always said—or something close to that.

Blanche picked up her project—a sock. "Surely by next winter the war will be over and our soldiers will be home."

"Surely," Vivian echoed, as if it were another prayer, this time out loud.

Two hours later, she had made the last stitch on the neck of the sleeveless sweater, tied it off, and securely woven in the ends. She would take it home to *block it—gently wash it then lay it out flat to dry into its final shape. Perhaps she and the girls could all lay a kiss on it before she mailed it off.*

On her way home, she followed a black car up the road to the farm. At first she barely noticed, but when it didn't turn right at the crossroads, a pit grew in her stomach. As they neared the farm, she began to chant quietly, "Please don't turn. Please don't turn."

But it did. It pulled to a stop to the right of the house. She parked beside it, but the Western Union man had already climbed out of the car.

She opened the pickup door, calling out, "Wait!"

He turned.

"I'm Vivian Connor." Her knees shook. "Do you have a telegram for me?"

He nodded.

Her knees nearly buckled as she placed one hand on the hood of the pickup. The man came closer, his hand extended.

Vivian took the telegram and opened it.

THE SECRETARY OF WAR DESIRES ME TO EXPRESS HIS DEEPEST REGRET THAT YOUR HUSBAND SGT EARL G CONNOR WAS KILLED IN ACTION IN DEFENSE OF HIS COUNTRY ON TWENTY-THIRD MARCH IN TUNISIA. Stop LETTER TO FOLLOW—

Still holding the telegram, she pushed against the truck as if bracing herself for what was to come, for her entire future.

"Are you all right, ma'am? Is there anything I can do to help?"

No. *She wasn't all right. Tears flooded her eyes. She stood and turned toward him, grateful for his kindness.* "My in-laws are here with me. I'm not alone." *They and her four children were with her. She would never be alone. But she would spend the rest of her life without Earl.*

CHAPTER FOURTEEN

*A*ll through church Debbie struggled to listen to the sermon, her mind consumed with thoughts of Vivian finding out that Earl had been killed in combat. Debbie's heart hurt for the young woman, even though it had all taken place over eighty years ago. It made her think of her own loss, of her fiancé Reed, an Army captain who'd been captured in Afghanistan and killed. The months after his death were the worst of her life, and she didn't have four young children to care for.

After church, Greg said he needed to leave to take Julian to a friend's house. "I'll pick you up at two," he said. "To go up to the farm." He turned to leave but then pivoted. "Any reason you're quiet today?"

"Am I?"

He nodded.

She sighed. "I've been thinking about your grandmother. I read more of her diary and letters last night, from the time your grandfather was killed in action. She had four little kids…" Debbie's voice trailed off. "I mean, I knew all of that, but to piece her story together from her diary and letters and photos makes it all feel so real."

Greg took her hand. "Thank you for doing that."

"I'm glad to do it." She paused a moment and then said, "It makes me wish I'd known your grandmother."

"She was a wonderful person."

"I can tell." Debbie made a shooing motion. "Go. We'll talk more about it later."

Spotting her parents across the foyer, she joined them, giving each of them a long hug. As she released her mother, Mom asked, "What's up?"

Debbie smiled. "I'm just feeling extra grateful for the two of you today."

When Greg picked Debbie up later, Sally and Paulette were already in the back seat of his truck. As they drove, Debbie told Sally about Liana's text. "She thinks the wool may have come from Europe." Debbie glanced back at Sally. "Can you think of how your dad would have come across yarn from Europe in North Africa?"

Sally shrugged. "Sure. Someone could have transported the yarn to North Africa from Europe. Maybe someone gave it to him, or maybe he bought it in a shop or from a local."

It didn't make sense. "And then Ted carried it for three years, all the way from Tunisia?"

"I know it's odd, and odd that I'd remember it. But I was an inquisitive little girl. I wanted to know everything, and I mean everything. I was Mama's helper, and I took my position seriously. Still do." She laughed. "Grandma Mary used to call me Little Miss Quizzical."

When they reached the farm, Sally said, "The house is vacant right now, I heard through the grapevine, so we don't need to worry about disturbing anyone. Let's stand on the porch."

Greg took Sally's arm, and Debbie took Paulette's. As they walked slowly to the porch, Debbie thought of Vivian walking from her truck to the front door. What a task she had ahead of her to tell Earl's parents that their only child had been killed. What a task to tell her children their father was dead. In that moment, the trajectory of all their lives changed forever.

Sally pointed at the barn. "Daddy worked so hard on that building, replacing the shingles a few at a time and the rotten boards. One of my first memories is of watching him do the work." She pointed to a chicken coop. "He made that when they first bought the farm. My mother told us the stories many times." Sally reached for Paulette's hand. "EJ was a lot like Daddy, as far as thinking ahead and trying to do right for his family, even if they never laid eyes on each other. In this earthly life, anyway."

"It's such a shame EJ never knew his father," Paulette said. "That would have meant everything to him. Thankfully Vivian and Ted did their best to fill that hole—for all of you, I know."

"Yes, yes they did," Sally said. "Ted was a good father to us—we couldn't have asked for anyone better than him." She brushed at her face. "Except for Daddy."

"Do you have any other memories of your father?" Greg asked.

She stood a little taller. "Well, he was handsome as can be. You've seen the photos. Movie-star handsome, especially in his uniform. And he loved to dance. He used to put a stack of albums on the phonograph—mostly swing music. Then he and Mama would start dancing. Often they'd wait until we were in bed, but sometimes Daddy couldn't wait and then we'd all dance together. I doubt my sisters remember that, being so young, but I do." Her eyes shone as she spoke. "He adored Mama. Her mother was a little distant, as we would say now. I'm pretty sure she had depression, based on what Mama described later. Her father traveled for work and was a bit of a rose-colored-glasses type of person. But Daddy understood Mama—and deeply loved her. Ted loved her too, but theirs was a more mature love. Not that sparkly love that Mama and Daddy shared."

Debbie wondered if the love between Greg and her was more mature. No. It still felt sparkly to her.

"Thank you for sharing that." Greg unzipped his jacket enough to pull out a piece of paper. "I'd like to read Grandpa's obituary as we honor his life." Greg cleared his throat and read, "'Earl Gregory Connor was born in New Philadelphia, Ohio, in 1917 and moved to Dennison with his family in 1923. He graduated from Dennison High School in 1935 and married Vivian Olson in 1936. They had four children. Earl Sr. was inducted into the US Army in May of 1942 and died during the Battle of El Guettar in Tunisia on March 23, 1943. He is survived by his parents, William and Mary Connor, his wife, Vivian, and their four children, all under six years old.'"

They were all silent for a long moment, but then Paulette asked, "Sally, what do you remember about your father's funeral?"

"Nothing." Sally crossed her arms. "It's the oddest thing. I remember so many details from my childhood but nothing from around the time of Daddy's death. Not Mama telling me he was dead. Not my reaction. Not the funeral. Brant told me one time it was probably the trauma of it that wiped the memories away." Her arms dropped to her side. "I wish I could remember. I wish Mama would have talked about it through the years, like she did the good things. Then maybe I would."

Debbie put her arm around her. "I'm sorry."

"You wouldn't think it would matter more than eighty years later, but it does. I never got over losing him."

"Of course not," Debbie said.

"I always wished I'd known Grandpa Earl," Greg said. "And I wish my boys could have been here today. Grandpa Ted was an amazing father and grandfather. But Grandpa Earl's death was such a loss to the family. That's why we want to honor him today, right? We don't want to forget him. He died to free the world from fascism. His sacrifice along with so many other soldiers helped turn the war around so the Allies could invade Europe."

"Yes." Sally exhaled. "Every word of that is true. I'm eternally grateful to Daddy and all those who served during World War II. They saved us all."

Once they were back in the truck, Debbie pulled a container of Janet's mini chocolate cupcakes with salted caramel topping from her bag. "I brought treats in honor of Earl's birthday. Janet made them yesterday afternoon before she left."

Paulette reached forward and patted Debbie's shoulder. "Thank you."

After they all ate one of the cupcakes, Debbie passed around wet wipes, and then Greg backed out of the driveway, onto the road.

Sally gasped. "Oh, I just thought of something."

"What?" Paulette asked.

"Debbie," Sally said, "you should ask Meg about the yarn. She's an expert."

"Meg? Who's Meg?"

"Meg Sinclair. She bought the property after Mama died."

"Meg Sinclair?" Debbie glanced at Greg and then back at Sally. "Meg is our dancing instructor."

"Oh, I didn't know she still did that," Sally said. "She raises sheep for wool." She pointed toward a half shed. "They're right there."

Debbie peered out her window. What appeared to be thirty sheep huddled together near a shed next to a red barn. "Meg Sinclair bought your mother's place?"

Greg shook his head. "I had no idea."

"Nor did I," Paulette added.

"Yes," Sally said. "She and her husband had bought the property next door around five years before Mama passed away."

"So how come no one is living in Vivian's house now?" Debbie asked.

"They're working on it," Sally said. "Meg has rented it out all these years, but she's between tenants and has been painting and doing updates. She said the new renters will move in soon. I asked about us going in today, but she said she has ladders and paint and equipment spread throughout the house." Sally shrugged. "That's understandable. She said I could come out and see it after she finishes the painting. Anyway, contact Meg about the yarn. See what she says. I have her number back in my room."

"I might have her number already." Debbie took out her phone and clicked on an email from Meg. "Yes, it's here in a message about the dance class. I'll give her a call in the morning."

After Greg dropped Sally and then Paulette off, he turned to Debbie. "Want to go to Pittsburgh with me?"

Debbie couldn't hide the surprise in her voice. "Now?"

"Yes. I have an appointment with an appraiser, a woman who specializes in antique jewelry." He patted his jacket pocket. "I have the ring with me."

It was an hour-and-a-half drive.

Greg added, "We can have dinner before we head home."

"What about the boys?"

"Julian is staying at his friend's until eight, and Jaxon is studying for a biology test."

Debbie leaned back against the seat. "Why not? Let's go to Pittsburgh."

As Greg drove south to Highway 22, Debbie asked how he found out about the appraiser. "Dad's cousin Katherine recommended her," he said.

A little alarmed, Debbie asked, "Is she a friend of Katherine's?"

"Yes." He shot Debbie a smile. "Don't worry. I asked the jeweler in Uhrichsville if he'd heard of her. He has—in fact, he said he should have thought of her in the first place."

They soon turned east. The road was clear, but snow dusted the sporadic woods, and ice hung from the branches of the trees. The afternoon sun bounced off the farmland, sending sparkles across the landscape.

Greg cleared his throat. Debbie expected him to say something, but then he didn't. She asked about his work.

"I got a bid for another remodel," he answered. "It'll be worth it but will mean juggling our schedules even more."

"I'm happy to help," Debbie said. "I can pick the boys up from practice when you can't."

"Thanks." He stared straight ahead. "It's good to have a backup plan. I'm looking forward to Jaxon getting his license sometime soon."

Pittsburgh had even more snow, including gray piles along the roadways and in parking lots studded with gravel from sanding the roads. Traffic got heavier as Greg made his way downtown, near Point State Park. Parking was scarce, and the sidewalks were crowded with people. They found a parking garage and then headed past restaurants and boutique shops to the appraiser's.

Greg opened the door, and Debbie stepped inside.

A woman sitting at a desk behind the counter stood. "May I help you?"

Greg moved forward. "I'm Greg Connor. I have an appointment with Elizabeth Barnes."

"Greg." The woman extended her hand across the counter. "So nice to meet you."

"This is my girlfriend, Debbie Albright," Greg said, shaking Elizabeth's hand.

Elizabeth extended her hand to Debbie next. "Nice to meet you too." After she let go of Debbie's hand, she said, "I'm looking forward to seeing the ring."

Greg took the box from his pocket and set it on the counter. "I'd appreciate knowing how much it's worth along with anything else you can determine—where and when it was made, that sort of thing."

"Absolutely." Elizabeth motioned to a table with a coffee maker and a water cooler. "Make yourselves at home. It should take a half hour or so." She gestured to the glass case on the far wall where light bounced off diamond after diamond after diamond. "Make sure to look at my collection. Each of those pieces has been handpicked by me—all have exquisite diamonds or other jewels and unique settings."

Greg ventured over to one case and peered inside.

Debbie went to another. Her eyes were immediately drawn to a white gold ring with three round-cut diamonds, the middle one just a little larger than the other two. The description included the date, 1919. Next to it was a brooch made of yellow gold, with a lovely set of ruby and diamond tulips, dated 1887. Each piece was absolutely unique. No prices were included. Debbie could only imagine what each cost.

Greg seemed engrossed in the display of antique pocket watches he was examining.

The next item in Debbie's case nearly took her breath away. She glanced over at Greg, but he didn't seem to have noticed. The label on the ring read: *1 ct. diamond with 12 round natural diamond accents, 18c gold; 1905.*

It was probably the loveliest ring she'd ever seen. A sparkling snowflake made of gold and diamonds set on a simple band. She let her mind drift on thoughts of who the original owner might have been, what her story was. She hoped it had been a happy one.

"Want a cup of coffee?" Greg called out from across the room. Debbie turned toward him, her reverie broken. Which was probably for the best.

"Sure," she said. Greg poured a cup of coffee for each of them, and they sat on the bench.

"I still can't believe Grandma had a ring like that." Greg's gaze drifted over to Elizabeth, who was sitting at her desk again, reading something on her computer screen. "I know I've said it before. Grandma appreciated quality, but nothing she had was fancy." He shook his head.

Debbie kept her voice low. "And to think she kept it in an old ball of yarn in her bottom drawer."

Greg laughed. "That must have felt normal to her kids who knew about it. But I guess that's part of childhood, feeling like the weird stuff in your family is actually quite normal."

Debbie grinned. "I guess so."

"I'm glad Dad had his siblings. I always wondered what that would be like. He mentioned once that his mom talked about how she always wanted to have a lot of kids." Greg leaned forward a little. "When he told me that, I asked why he and Mom didn't have more kids. He said they wanted to, but it just didn't happen."

"I've completed the appraisal," Elizabeth said, placing a black velvet board on the counter next to a book.

Greg and Debbie stood and joined her at the counter.

"I've seen a ring similar to this before, which gave me a head start. It originated in Rome sometime between 1880 and 1885, toward the end of the Grand Victorian Period, and was made by a well-known Italian designer, Antonio Buccellati. It is a ten-carat cushion-cut diamond. The antique shape and older style of cutting disguises its true brilliance. I can only guess at what it's worth." She then quoted a number that made them both gasp.

"Do you think the ring came directly from Italy to the US?" Greg asked.

"There's no way to tell," Elizabeth said. "There was a lot of jewelry trade around Europe at that time, plus wealthy Americans were taking tours of Europe and purchasing jewelry to bring home."

"Is there any way to figure out when the ring came to the US?"

"Unfortunately, no. Unless there's documentation of it being appraised before now. Do any jewelers in your area have a record of it?"

"Not that we can find," Greg said. "The jeweler I took it to asked around, but none of the jewelers in the area had seen it before. So not at least in the last few decades."

"There are all sorts of possibilities. Someone bought it in Europe on a grand tour and brought it over. Someone immigrated and brought it." She shrugged. "Who knows? That said, it at one time belonged to someone of means. If you'd like to sell it today, I'll give you $65,000."

"I'm not interested in selling it," Greg said. "But thank you for the information."

"I don't blame you for keeping it." Elizabeth grinned at Greg and then Debbie. "I'll contact you if I come across any additional information."

Greg paid for the appraisal, and Elizabeth put the ring in the box and handed it to Greg, who put it back in his pocket and zipped it. Elizabeth smiled at Debbie again. "It really is a beautiful ring."

Did Elizabeth think Greg intended to give the ring to her? Debbie's face grew warm. She managed to echo Elizabeth, saying, "It really is."

They found a Mediterranean café for an early dinner on the way back to the parking garage. As they ate bread and baba ghanoush, tabbouleh, kebabs, and kofta, Greg kept turning the conversation back to the ring, even though it was an uncomfortable topic for Debbie. She didn't want him to think she expected it. In fact, that was what made her feel uncomfortable.

Did she love Greg Connor? Yes. Did she want to marry him? She had to admit that she did. But she didn't want him to think she was after his grandmother's ring. And she definitely wasn't. It was lovely, but it didn't suit her personality or lifestyle.

"I'm trying to figure out what to do with it," Greg said. "The ring doesn't belong to me. If it did come from the Johnston family, then it probably should go to Katherine. If Sally is right and it was in Grandpa's possession for a time, and her mother intended it for her—and we have no proof she didn't—then it should go to her. Or at least to her and her remaining siblings."

Relieved that he didn't seem to think she wanted it, Debbie said, "You'll know what to do with it when we figure out where it came from—and where it's been."

On the way home, Debbie had a text from Katherine. I'VE BEEN DOING SOME RESEARCH. IT LOOKS AS IF THE RING WAS DESIGNED BY AN ITALIAN GOLDSMITH IN ROME, ANTONIO BUCCELLATI. MY GRANDMOTHER WAS ITALIAN! SHE CAME TO THE US IN 1895, AS A YOUNG WOMAN. HER ITALIAN FAMILY WAS QUITE WEALTHY, AS WAS MY GRANDFATHER'S FAMILY HERE IN THE STATES. I THINK WE'VE FOUND OUR MISSING LINK!

Debbie groaned.

"What's up?" Greg asked.

Debbie read him the text.

Greg frowned. "Do you think Elizabeth and Katherine have been talking?"

"Wouldn't that be a conflict of interest? For you to pay for an appraisal only to have Elizabeth share the information with a relative?"

"It doesn't seem very professional."

Greg's phone rang. Debbie glanced at his control screen. *Elizabeth Barnes.* That was quick. Greg hit accept and said, "Hello."

"Greg, it's Elizabeth. I wanted to let you know that I just got off the phone with Katherine. She begged me for details, but I refused to discuss the ring with her. However, she'd already come up with the same information I found. Someone must have given her a description—possibly a photograph. If she contacts you, I wanted to let you know that I didn't divulge any information to her."

Greg glanced at Debbie as he said, "Thank you for letting me know."

"Make sure to get in touch if you have any questions."

After Greg ended the call, Debbie asked, "How should I reply to Katherine?"

"Don't," Greg said. "She shouldn't have contacted you. If she wants to talk to me about the ring, she can text me."

Debbie asked, "How do you think Katherine got a picture of the ring?"

"Remember Sally took one that Sunday at your house?" Greg asked. "She probably texted it to Lottie, who passed it on to Katherine."

Debbie leaned back against the seat as her phone dinged. This time it was Janet. Do you have a minute?

"It's Janet," Debbie said to Greg. She texted back, saying she was on the way back from Pittsburgh with Greg.

Pittsburgh! Whatever for?

Debbie replied, KIND OF A LONG STORY. HOW ABOUT IF I CALL WHEN I'M HOME? UNLESS WHAT YOU WANTED TO TALK ABOUT IS URGENT?

IT CAN WAIT. TALK TO YOU LATER.

The sun set off to the west in one of those beautiful Ohio displays of color, shooting orange and pink streaks through wispy clouds across the horizon. Soon it was pitch-dark except for the headlights of the pickup on the road and the occasional vehicle coming toward them. The moon rose, and a few stars began to shine. Then more.

Debbie reached over and turned up the radio, which was tuned to a '70s station. A familiar song was playing, so they both began to sing. By the time they arrived back in Dennison, Debbie's voice was hoarse. But she was happy.

As Greg parked in front of her house, she said, "Thank you for a wonderful adventure."

"Anytime." They exited the car then walked hand in hand up to her front door.

After a kiss good night, she said, "Call me in the morning?"

"Or tonight?"

She laughed. "*And* tonight."

Once she was inside, she called Janet, who picked up before the first ring ended. "Why did you and Greg go to Pittsburgh?"

"We took Vivian's ring for an appraisal."

Janet gasped. "Sorry, I just heard the word *ring*. Nothing else."

Debbie laughed as she hung her purse on the hook in her closet. "Vivian's."

"Oh." Janet paused. "Is he planning to give it to you?"

"No," she said firmly. "He wants it to go to whoever *should* have it—which isn't him, and it especially isn't me." She wiggled out of her coat. "But I did have an awkward moment with the appraiser. Greg had introduced me as his girlfriend."

"As he should."

Debbie hung up her coat. "Right, but there was a pause when she implied the ring was for me. Neither Greg nor I said anything."

"But you don't know that Greg was feeling the same way you were? Awkward?"

"True. I'm just wondering now if he did." Debbie kicked off her boots and put them in the closet as she spoke. "He crossed his arms. Then took a step sideways, away from me."

"Hmm. Interesting. Well, don't read too much into it," Janet said. "Sometimes it's hard to know what to say in that kind of situation—sometimes it's better not to say anything at all. Why don't you ask him how he felt?"

Debbie chuckled as she stopped at the dining room table. "What a novel idea."

"Isn't it?" Janet laughed. "I'm always available for relationship advice. So what did the appraiser say about Vivian's ring?"

"It was made by a famous designer in Rome between 1880 and 1885. It's worth a lot of money."

"Do you think it came from Vivian's family in England?"

Debbie began thumbing through Vivian's photographs and stopped at a photo of Vivian with an older woman who looked like her. "Charlotte's family?"

"That's her mother, right?"

"Yes." Debbie was certain the woman in the photo was Charlotte, although she hadn't noticed it before. "We haven't really explored that possibility. I suppose it might have."

"Ian has a cousin who is a jeweler in London at a super posh place. Do you want me to ask her if she knows of the designer and if his rings were common in England?"

"Sure." Debbie sat at the table and pulled Vivian's diary close. "The more information we can track down, the better. And now I'll say good night. I'm going to read more of Vivian's own words before bed."

CHAPTER FIFTEEN

Connor Farm, Dennison, Ohio
March 31, 1943

As Vivian stepped onto the porch, she barely registered Will as he strode up from the barn. With the telegram still in her hand, Vivian glanced at the window, where Mary stood inside. For a moment their eyes locked and both women froze, but then Mary slipped out the front door, pulling it shut behind her, just as Will reached them. Vivian handed him the telegram and fell into the arms of her mother-in-law.

"I'm sorry," Vivian wailed. "I'm so sorry. Your only living child."

"Your husband." Mary began to shake as she hugged Vivian. "Cry it out now. Lottie and EJ are napping, and the big girls are in their room playing with their dolls."

Will wrapped his arms around them both.

Vivian cried some more and then dried her tears. A cold wind blew, but she barely felt it. Mary shivered beside her. They needed to go inside.

"What do I tell the girls?" Vivian asked.

"Tell them their daddy has gone to heaven," Mary said. "Tell them we're all sad, but we will be okay, including them. Tell them that you and Grandpa Will and I will take good care of them."

That seemed wise. Vivian squeezed Mary's hand.

"When they're older, tell them more."

Vivian did as her mother-in-law instructed. Carol kept on playing while Sally's face went slack. Vivian expected her to cry, wanted her to cry, but instead Sally climbed into her bed and pulled the covers over her head. Vivian sat beside her and rubbed her back.

"What's wrong with her?" Carol asked.

"She's sad," Vivian replied.

"Oh," was all Carol said as she turned back to her baby sister and the dollhouse Earl had made two summers before.

An hour later, Vivian sat down in the rocking chair near the woodstove with EJ. A knock sounded on the door. Mary answered it, speaking in a low voice. There was a muffled response. Vivian couldn't make out who was at the door or what was being said. Perhaps the nearest neighbors had seen the Western Union car.

But then her mother, followed by her father, stepped into the living room. She wore her red wool coat and hat.

"My darling." Mum swept across the living room.

Vivian stood, moving EJ to her shoulder as she did. Mum didn't hug her, but she did put her hands on Vivian's arms and looked her in the eyes. "I'm so sorry."

Her father joined them and gave Vivian, along with EJ, a gentle hug. Mum then took the baby in her arms. Carol and Lottie came out of the bedroom and clung to Vivian's skirt. "It's Grannie and Grandpa," Carol whispered to Lottie, who didn't seem to remember her maternal grandparents.

Vivian's father asked, "Is Will out in the barn?"

"Yes," Mary answered. "Or perhaps working on the pasture fence."

"I'll go out and say hello," Daddy said.

"How did you find out so quickly?" Vivian asked her mother as the two sat side by side on the sofa.

"Mary called the depot and managed to talk to your father directly."

Vivian glanced at her mother-in-law, who was now at the table with Carol and Lottie, giving them glasses of milk. She was grateful Mary had made the call.

Vivian hadn't overheard Mary's conversation with Daddy. She must have been in the bedroom with the girls. Mary never commented on Vivian's relationship with her parents, but she knew they needed to know Earl had been killed and had done so with her usual quiet efficiency. Vivian was so numb, she hadn't even thought of making the call herself.

"Where's Sally?" Mum asked.

"In her bed. I think she understands." Vivian lowered her voice. "Carol and Lottie don't."

Mum nodded. "Daisy understood immediately when her father passed away." EJ stirred, and Mum gently patted his back as if she cared for him every day, instead of this being the first time she'd ever held him. "Daisy retained her gregarious personality, but she never got over her father's death." Mum's mouth turned down a little. "Neither did I."

Vivian shifted toward her mother. Not once had Mum ever spoken about her first husband in front of Vivian.

Balancing EJ with one hand, Mum patted Vivian's leg. "I truly am so sorry, darling. I know how much you loved—" She broke off. "Love Earl. He was good to you and the children, and a good son to his parents. He will be missed greatly." Tears filled Mum's eyes—something else Vivian had never witnessed before.

"I won't tell you to have a stiff upper lip about this business. It's impossible. But I will tell you it will get better in time. You'll adjust. You'll care for your children. You'll continue to mourn. And perhaps, in time, another man worthy of your love will come into your life. But none of what may come in the future can make what you're going through now easier. My only advice is to do your best to take life a day at a time. Don't look too far ahead. That's what I tried to do."

Mum hadn't given Vivian advice for years, not since she begged her not to marry Earl when she was eighteen.

Daddy and Will came in with several bags of groceries.

Mum said, "We stopped by the store on the way here. We didn't want you to have to think about grocery shopping anytime soon."

"Thank you." Vivian fought back tears again. "For everything."

Earl's service was held on a Friday afternoon, two weeks later, at the Community Church. The sanctuary overflowed with mourners.

Vivian recognized friends of Earl and herself from high school. Some in attendance were from church.

She'd been told all the knitting circle women would be there. Others were friends of Earl's parents, people who worked with Vivian's father, or neighbors of her parents. But many were people Vivian had never seen before.

All wanted to honor Earl.

As she sat in the front pew with the baby in her arms, Sally pulled Lottie onto her lap. Carol stepped over Vivian's feet and sat on the other side. Her precious girls and baby boy. Mum had suggested the children not go to the funeral, but Vivian insisted they be with her. Perhaps only Sally would remember the service, but Vivian didn't want to tell them years later that she'd left them at home that day. Besides, who would they feel comfortable staying with? No one.

Vivian fought her tears as the pastor read Psalm 23 and then opened in prayer. When EJ began to fuss, Mum took him and patted his back, gently swaying until he fell asleep. Pastor Wilkinson spoke of Earl's service to his country. "We all knew how hard it was for him to leave his family behind," he said. "But he was willing to go, to do his part to right our world. We'll be forever indebted to his sacrifice and to the sacrifices of his dear wife and four young children."

He went on to speak about the resurrection and the hope of heaven, focusing on John 14:1–6. "Let not your heart be troubled: ye believe in God, believe also in me. In my Father's house are many mansions: if it were not so, I would have told you. I go to prepare a place for you..."

Vivian's comfort was that Earl was now at peace. No more war. No more sorrow. But how her heart ached for him—and for her family's future. Would she be able to keep the farm?

After the sermon, the pastor read the eulogy. Vivian had tried to write it, but finally her in-laws took over the task. Pastor Wilkinson read about Earl's early life, about losing his older sister to the Spanish flu, about his arrival in Dennison. "And then, at the beginning of his senior year of high school, Earl met the love of his life."

Vivian closed her eyes.

"A young woman from London, Vivian Olson, had moved to our little town. Earl was smitten and told his parents that night that he'd met someone special. The two soon started dating and then married after graduation. Together they farmed the land Earl purchased on Hickory Road. They welcomed their first child, Sally Rose—"

Vivian put her arm around Sally and pulled her close, but her oldest daughter kept her eyes on her little sister's head.

"—in 1938. Carol joined the family in 1940, and Charlotte arrived in 1942. Earl Jr was born just over a month ago. Earl Connor Sr. is survived by his beloved wife and children, his mother and father, Mary and William Connor, his in-laws, Charlotte and Richard Olson, and many friends."

After he finished the service, Pastor Wilkinson said, "There will be no burial today, but we will gather on the lawn of the church for a twenty-one-gun salute. Then please join the family in the fellowship hall for refreshments."

As Vivian stood, her knees buckled, and Mum, still holding EJ, reached over Carol and looped her free arm through Vivian's. Then she passed the baby to Daddy and walked with Vivian, guiding Carol to go on ahead with Sally, Lottie, Mary, and Will. In the last two weeks, Mum had been the mother Vivian had always longed for.

They gathered on the church lawn, under the oak tree. The snow had melted, and the day was warm, although snow threatened. As the seven soldiers who had traveled from Akron shot their rifles into the air in honor of Earl, Sally and Carol put their hands over their ears. At first Vivian thought Mary was reaching down to comfort them, but then she realized her mother-in-law was falling as the last of the shots rang out. Was the grief *too much for her? Vivian lunged to the side, trying to catch her as Will grabbed his wife's arm. But she slumped to the ground, her eyes closed and her body limp.*

Vivian left the pickup with Will at the hospital that afternoon, and Mum and Daddy took her and the children back to the farm. Mum put together a light supper and then put the girls to bed. Daddy went with Vivian out to the barn and fed the livestock as she milked the cow. She sent him in with the bucket of milk and asked him to carry more wood into the house. After feeding the chickens and gathering the eggs, she went into the house too. Mum had done the dishes and cleaned the kitchen.

"Call and let us know how Mary is," Mum said. "I'll have Daddy bring me out here in the morning before he goes to work."

"I don't go out of town until next week," Daddy said.

Vivian hugged her parents goodbye.

Mum said, "I'm praying for Mary."

"Thank you." Vivian had never been so thankful for her mother. Somehow, she'd risen to the occasion to meet Vivian and the children's needs. Perhaps it was because she remembered the grief of being a young

widow. Perhaps it was a mother's love. Whatever it was, Mum had made Vivian her only priority.

Vivian put on her nightgown and robe, and then, after feeding EJ, sat down by the woodstove and picked up her knitting that she hadn't touched in two weeks. She only had the ribbing to finish on the sleeveless sweater. Perhaps she could finish it tonight.

The letter she'd received from the army had said Earl was buried in Tunisia. She would be notified, in time, exactly where. She longed for his body to be returned to her but guessed that it would be nearly impossible to ship the bodies of the dead home, especially when the fighting raged on. Resources were needed to fight the Italians and the Germans. That was how it should be, but it broke her heart all over again to think of Earl buried half a world away.

She knitted and rocked, her mind flitting from one thing to another.

Finally, she took a few deep breaths, allowing the rhythm of the needles and the warmth of the fire in the stove to soothe here. Vivian prayed for them all, and said a special prayer for her mother-in-law.

Dr. Roy had been at Earl's service and immediately rushed to Mary's side. Four younger men had picked her up and carried her to the doctor's car. He took her to the hospital with Will holding her in the back seat.

Just after ten o'clock, Vivian finished the sleeve-less sweater and put it in her knitting bag. She started toward her bedroom just as the front door opened. Will stepped inside, nose and cheeks red from the cold wind that blew outside.

"How is she?" Vivian asked.

"Better," he answered. "Doc said she's had a stroke. Her speech is affected some, and the use of her right hand. She'll be in the hospital for a few days." He hung up his coat. "She feels horrible that she inter-rupted Earl's service."

Tears sprang to Vivian's eyes. "You tell her to feel no such thing. Tell her we're relieved she's alive."

Will ran his hand through his thick gray hair. Vivian would never know Earl as a fifty-three-year-old man. Never know him as a grandfather. Never know him as an old man.

"She doesn't want to be a burden," Will said.

"Mary will never be a burden." But no doubt their lives would change again. Vivian would have to figure out how to help Will with the farming, care for the chil-dren, and care for Mary too.

But she'd do it. She had to.

CHAPTER SIXTEEN

onday morning was extra slow at the café, so just after ten
Debbie texted the number she had for Meg, explaining who she
was and that she wanted to speak with her about a knitting project that
had belonged to Vivian Olson Connor Johnston. SALLY SAID YOU'RE
AN EXPERT ON WOOL AND YARN. I'M HOPING YOU CAN HELP ME.

Debbie didn't get a reply until after she'd finished closing the café.
SORRY. JUST SAW THIS. I'M WORKING ON THE INTERIOR OF THE OLD
JOHNSTON HOUSE THIS AFTERNOON. WANT TO STOP BY? YOU COULD
SEE THE INSIDE OF THE HOUSE IF YOU'D LIKE. WE COULD CHAT THEN.

THANK YOU! Debbie texted back. I'LL BE OUT IN A HALF HOUR
OR SO.

She stopped by her house and picked up the ball of yarn, knitting
needles, and scarf. She wouldn't mention the ring to Meg. It was
Greg's family's business, and the fewer people who knew about it,
the better.

When Debbie arrived back at the farm, there was a new late
model Ford pickup with bed rails and racks parked in the driveway.
A metal ladder was on the racks, and the bed held several totes.

Excited to see the inside of the house, Debbie hurried up the
front steps to the porch where she'd recently stood. She knocked on
the door.

"It's open," a muffled voice called out. "Come on in."

Debbie opened the door and stepped inside.

"I'm in the living room."

She stepped through the entryway into the living room. It was all much bigger and brighter than she imagined. The walls were getting a fresh coat of paint, and there were no coverings on the windows.

"Debbie." Meg, who had a scarf tied over her hair and wore overalls, climbed down the ladder. "So nice to see you." She wiped her hands on a rag. "I wondered if your dancing partner—Greg, right?"

Debbie nodded.

"I wondered if he was related to the Connor family that used to own this place," Meg said. "It appears he is."

"That's right," Debbie said. "His grandmother was Vivian."

"Then I must have known Greg when he was a little boy. I've forgotten Vivian's grandsons' names—there were two that were around."

"Yes, Greg and Sally's son, Brant. Greg was EJ's son. His mom is Paulette."

"You know, now that I'm giving it some thought, those names ring a bell. I was around quite a bit in Vivian's final years and have kept in touch with Sally. We moved next door before Ted died."

"You mentioned your sheep at dance class on Saturday, but I didn't have any idea you lived up this way or owned this place until yesterday after we all gathered here to honor Earl. Sally pointed out your sheep after we left."

"Yes, I raise sheep for their wool. I started right after Vivian passed away. I already knew how to knit, but Vivian inspired me to do more of it." She glanced at the bag. "What do you have for me?"

Debbie took the knitting project out of the bag. "I'm curious about the yarn used in this project. We found it in a box of Vivian's things. Sally said you're an expert when it comes to wool. I'm hoping you might have an opinion."

"Oh, I'm no expert."

"But you raise sheep for their wool."

"I do."

"And you've traveled to Europe on wool tours."

"Only one," Meg said.

"I hope you can give me some idea of where this came from." She extended the project to Meg.

But the woman held up her hands. "I should wash up first." She waved to her right. "Come see the rest of the house. You can put the yarn down by the woodstove."

The entire house was empty. They walked through the dining room and turned to the left toward the kitchen. "I've done a lot of work on the place through the years," Meg said. "I redid the kitchen before the previous renters moved in. About five years ago."

"It's beautiful," Debbie said. The cabinets were white, the counters were granite, and the floor was a gray tile. "What a wonderful rental property."

"I used to think we'd move in here when we had a family. It's bigger than our house, but Jeff and I were never blessed that way. It's been rewarding to be able to rent it out to other families."

"How well did you know Vivian?"

"Very well." Meg smiled as she led the way through the second kitchen door that connected back to the entryway. "She was like a favorite aunt to me." She led the way down the hall.

"Did you ever find anything from the family through the years? Anything they left behind?"

Meg laughed. "I used to find little green army men in the flower beds, but I'm guessing those were left behind by Greg and his cousin."

Debbie laughed too. "You're probably right."

Meg pointed to a large room. "This is a family room now—I knocked out what was the nursery and expanded the room—but it used to be Vivian and Ted's room. When we bought the farm, the house had six bedrooms, but over the years I've remodeled it down to four. I combined two other rooms for a suite with a bathroom and a little sitting room. It's upstairs."

She stopped at the next door. "Here's the main floor bathroom. I'm going to wash my hands here." She kept talking as she washed. "I was already interested in knitting when we bought the place next door. Jeff had inherited money from his grandparents, which allowed us to buy more land than we'd expected to be able to. We were young, in our mid-twenties. Vivian took me under her wing and taught me all sorts of things. Canning. Sewing. Cooking. And more about knitting than I'd learned from my own grandmother. She really sparked my interest, far more than she knew."

They continued with the tour. The house was bigger than Debbie had realized from Vivian's diary or from what she'd seen of it from the outside. No wonder Vivian had wanted to have a dozen children. There were two bedrooms downstairs, and then upstairs was the suite, another bedroom, and a small bathroom. Meg pointed out the window of the landing. "That's my house."

It was smaller but appeared good-sized on its own.

"Let's go take a look at the yarn," Meg said. "Just in case I happen to know anything about it."

When they reached the living room, Meg picked up the bag and pulled out the contents. Holding the ball with one hand and the scarf with the other, she tugged the scarf tight. "This is interesting. It looks as if it could be a sampler. I'm guessing Lottie did it. Vivian told me she was the only one of the girls who took up knitting."

"Someone else told me they thought it was a sampler, but then someone else said the stitching was odd."

Meg looked closer. "It is odd. And the yarn is old, and definitely hand spun."

"Any idea how old?"

Meg ran her hand over the scarf. "Decades, for sure."

"How about where the yarn is from?"

"It's not from around here," Meg said. "Perhaps the Northeast."

"Or Europe?"

"It could be," Meg answered. "You said it was with Vivian's things?"

"Yes." Debbie clasped her hands together.

"Well, I'm guessing it was some quirky project Lottie did, probably from some old yarn that Vivian acquired somehow. Isn't Lottie still alive? Have you asked her?"

"Yes, she's still alive. But, no, I haven't asked her. I will."

Meg pulled out the knitting needle from the ball of yarn. "The needles are ancient too, aren't they?"

"They appear to be. That's what I've been told, anyway."

Meg shook her head. "I don't remember Vivian having anything like these." She put the project back into Debbie's bag then handed it to Debbie. "I hope someone else will be able to help you more than I can. Sorry, I don't have much to offer."

"That's all right." Debbie tucked the bag under her arm. "Thank you for trying, and thank you for the tour. It's been a delight to see the house."

Meg smiled. "This home has always had good vibes. Vivian poured so much love into whoever entered it, even when she was dying. And then her kids, Sally and EJ in particular, took such good care of her when she was ill."

Debbie thought about Vivian's diary as she walked out to her car. On the night of Earl's funeral, Vivian feared she couldn't survive, couldn't stay on the farm. But she had. So much so that the young neighbor woman she mentored could feel Vivian's love—and the love of her children—all of these years later.

The next morning, Patricia, Harry, and Crosby came into the café right on time. As they shed their heavy coats, Debbie arrived at their table with a cup of black coffee for Harry. "Welcome," she said. "How are all of you today?"

"I can't complain." Harry patted Crosby's head. "Neither can Crosby."

"And I'm doing great," Patricia said. "Got a potential client to meet with today, so I need all the energy I can get."

"Wonderful," Debbie said. "I'll be right out with your mocha." She turned to Harry. "Do you want your regular breakfast?"

Harry nodded. "Yes, please."

When Debbie delivered their breakfasts—oatmeal for Patricia and eggs and toast for Harry, with an extra egg for Crosby—she said, "Harry, I really appreciated your memories of Vivian's parents. Do you remember Earl's parents?"

Harry put his coffee cup down. "Do you have a minute?"

She glanced around the café at the other customers, who seemed fine. She could take a couple of minutes. "Sure."

Once she pulled up a chair, Harry said, "I've been thinking about Will and Mary Connor since our last talk. They were good people too. He worked as a laborer mostly, but they saved enough to buy a small farm. Mrs. Connor took in laundry and sold eggs and milk. Of course, that was during the Depression. They were hard workers, like most people. They passed on that ethic to Earl." He reached down and patted Crosby's head. "I know I've said this before, but Earl and Vivian were quite the pair."

Debbie smiled at the image of the two as a power couple.

"Everyone knew who she was—the girl from England. She didn't have much of an accent though." Harry shrugged. "We all thought she'd come straight from England, but it turned out she'd been in the US for a few years."

"Yes," Debbie said. "Since she was ten. What do you remember about Will and Mary from the war years?"

"They rented out their place and moved in with Vivian to help with the kids. Then Mary had a stroke on the day of Earl's funeral. It seemed too much for that family—they'd had far more than their share of heartache. Will took Mary back to Vivian's place for a couple more years, and they all took care of her and the children and the farm together. Of course I didn't realize how young Vivian was at the time, but she was a super mom and daughter-in-law. There was a lot of love in that family."

A woman stepped into the café. Debbie called out a hello and said, "I'll be right with you." Then she placed her hand on Harry's arms. "Thank you. That was lovely."

And it confirmed what she had read so far in Vivian's diaries.

Debbie kept thinking about Harry's memories long after he, Crosby, and Patricia left. What she was hearing over and over was that Vivian was a strong, capable woman who, at the time of Earl's death, mothered her four children and cared for her mother-in-law and farm, all with a heart of love. Greg came from a strong family foundation, from Mary and Will. From Earl and Vivian. From EJ and Paulette.

Even Charlotte was turning out to have more character than Debbie first expected. Vivian's mother, despite her depression and worry about Daisy, rallied and helped Vivian after Earl's death.

That afternoon, as Debbie cleaned, her phone rang. It was Liana. Debbie accepted the call. After greeting each other, Liana said, "I heard back from my friend in Scotland. She found the sampler or scarf or whatever it was particularly interesting. She said this may be a long shot, but that you should look into female spies in France during World War II."

"What does knitting have to do with spies?"

"That's what I asked, but it turns out there was a group of women spying in France who knitted intelligence information into scarfs and sweaters and things like that."

Remembering that Vivian had knitted code into Earl's scarf, Debbie knew that was plausible. "Do you know how it worked, exactly?"

"No," Liana said. "I haven't had a chance to research it. But my friend, Alice, said it's worth looking into. You may have an example of that. Alice has a contact in France that may be able to help you."

"Does the contact in France speak English?"

"Yes," Liana said. "I'll text you the woman's email address. Her name is Marietta. Please let me know what you find out."

"Of course," Debbie answered.

Just after she ended the call, Liana's text came through. Debbie sat at the back table and composed an email to the woman. Then she attached several photos of the ball of yarn, the project, and the knitting needles. If the project was the work of a female spy, how would it have come into Earl's possession? Had he been involved in intelligence work?

After Debbie locked the door to the café, she headed through the lobby to the museum and made her way to Kim's office. She knocked, and after a long moment, Kim said, "Come in."

"Hi." Debbie put both hands on the chair across from Kim's desk. "How is Barry doing?"

"The same," Kim answered. "We're still waiting for more answers."

Debbie gave her hand a caring pat as she sat down. "I wanted to check about the photograph of Earl and the other soldiers. Did your photographer enlarge it?"

"Yes." Kim turned to her computer. "I have an email from him." She scrolled through to find it. "He enhanced the photo, and it looks like there's a pattern of what could be interpreted as dots and dashes on the scarf Earl is wearing. Three lines. The first line just has two dots—that's all. The scarf is twisted a little, so I'm not sure about the content of the other two lines.'"

"What are two dots in Morse code?" Debbie asked.

"The letter *I*," Kim answered.

Debbie smiled. "As in *I* love you."

Kim returned her smile. "Could be."

As Debbie left the depot, her phone dinged with a text from Janet. Sorry we didn't get a chance to talk today. Do you have a minute? I may have some pertinent information for you.

Debbie laughed and texted back, How mysterious of you.

Janet replied, I'll make hot chocolate. Just like my mother used to for us on a cold day after school. Come over?

On my way, Debbie responded.

Of course it wasn't regular old hot chocolate. It was French hot chocolate made with whole milk, bittersweet chocolate, and espresso powder.

"This is delicious." Debbie took a second sip. "So, what have you found out?"

Janet's eyes sparkled. "I found out about *the* ring accidentally—at least it could be *the* ring."

Debbie sat up straighter. "What? Where? How?"

"Yesterday, I was doing more research on Daisy Dumont Chapman but wasn't having much luck. I asked Ian's cousin, Annabel—who works at the jewelers in Europe—to see what she could find. She came up with an engagement announcement." Janet stood and stepped to her desk. She returned with a manila folder and then pulled out a piece of paper. "I printed it out for you."

"Thank you." Debbie stared at the announcement. There was a photo of a young woman with a dazzling smile and a dashing man, plus a short article.

> *Mr. Ronald Chapman announced the engagement of his oldest son, Mr. Noel Chapman, to Miss Daisy Dumont, at an engagement party held at the family home in Berkshire. Miss Dumont is the daughter of the late international business- man Luc Dumont and the granddaughter of Andre Dumont, owner of Dumont Textiles, of Paris. A family heirloom ring with a 10-carat cushion-cut diamond was presented to Miss Dumont by the young Mr. Chapman at the party. The mother of the bride is Mrs. Charlotte Dumont Olson.*

Debbie locked eyes with Janet. "Does it seem to you as if Charlotte was an afterthought?"

"Yes, it did," Janet said. "But focus on the ring. Didn't you say that the diamond is a 10-carat cushion cut?"

"Yeah." Debbie glanced down at the article. "It looks as if Daisy is wearing the ring in the photo."

"Really?" Janet leaned across the table.

Debbie pointed to the photo. "Is the electronic copy clearer?"

"No. I enlarged it and lightened it before I printed it," Janet said. "Ian's cousin found it in an online archive. The article had been photographed, I think—it wasn't good quality to start with."

Debbie took out her phone and used her magnifying app. Then she looked at the ring. "It's hard to tell if it's the same ring, but it's a big stone." She closed the app. "Too bad the announcement didn't specify if the ring was from the Chapman family or the Dumont family."

"I thought that too," Janet said. "I'm guessing it was the Chapman family."

"So am I." Debbie took a sip of the hot chocolate. "It was the Chapmans who placed the announcement, so it stands to reason they'd be bragging about their heirloom. Yet the Dumont family was wealthy."

"I got that impression too." Janet took another document out of the folder. "I did more research on them as well." She passed the document to Debbie. "It's in French, but I ran it through a translation app. It's not perfect, of course, but we can get the gist. It's an upper-class directory entry. Once Germany occupied France, the Nazis took control of the Dumonts' textile business and commissioned parachutes and uniforms. The Dumonts continued to operate the business though. The family had a home in Paris and a chateau in Normandy."

She passed another article toward Debbie. It too was in French. "Here's the basic translation. The grandfather, André, opened a branch of the business in Algiers, Algeria, with permission from the Vichy government. However, the family closed the branch after the Allied invasion of North Africa. By then the Nazis had commandeered their house in Paris. The youngest son took over the business and operated it after the war, but it was never as successful as before. He sold the business to a large corporation in 1961."

"Fascinating," Debbie said.

"Some of the women in the family went to the chateau in Normandy after the Paris house was confiscated by the Nazis."

"What's the source on that?"

"An article in a local newspaper. Annabel found it." Janet closed the file. "The printout is in here as well."

"Could we go back to Luc for a minute?" Debbie asked. "How did he and Charlotte meet?"

"It was a bit of a scandal. She was a London working girl—his secretary. They fell in love. It seems his family came to accept Charlotte, and they absolutely adored Daisy."

"Speaking of Daisy, have you found anything about her after 1942?"

Janet shook her head. "Annabel didn't either. But we'll keep looking."

"Her mother was afraid she went to France."

Janet wrinkled her nose. "I don't know that there are records of people traveling in and out of the country during the war. Or if we could find them, even if there were."

Debbie said, "It seems more likely, if she went, that she snuck in."

"Oh." Janet sucked in a breath. "That adds a level of intrigue, doesn't it?"

Debbie nodded.

Janet hesitated and then asked, "Would she take a ring like that into a war zone?"

"Maybe," Debbie answered. "She could use it to buy all sorts of supplies if needed. Or bribe her way out."

"Did Earl and Daisy ever meet?"

"Not that I know of," Debbie said. "And Earl died in North Africa, over a year before any US soldiers landed in France."

"Oh, that's right. But her family had a business branch in North Africa. What if she went there?"

Debbie thought for a moment. "Were civilians going to North Africa during the war?"

"Someone in her family did—or at least someone affiliated with the business."

Debbie couldn't imagine a woman going to North Africa in the midst of such horrific fighting.

Janet leaned forward. "Is this triggering for you, considering Reed's story?"

Debbie hesitated a moment. "You know, it's not any sadder than it would be anyway. Time doesn't heal all wounds—but it normalizes them." She shrugged. "I certainly know I'm not alone in my grief—nor in my progress to be able to live my life again." Debbie stood and took her mug to the sink. "Speaking of, I'm going to go home and look through more of Vivian's diaries."

CHAPTER SEVENTEEN

Connor Farm, Dennison, Ohio

May 3, 1943

Two weeks after Earl's funeral, one last letter arrived from him, dated a week before he was killed. It was a short note reminding Vivian of his love for her and the children. He included a photograph of himself and several other soldiers. Earl wore the scarf she'd made him. She detected a hole in the right lower side. The other soldiers wore T-shirts.

My buddy Ted is on the far right. He's from Chicago and went through Dennison on the train to boot camp. He's the brother I never had—I'm guessing he'll tire of hearing about you and the kids at some point, but so far he hasn't. Already, I trust him with my life.

He closed the letter with, Thank you for your prayers. Please continue. And please give Mom and Pop my love—tell them I'll write soon. Kiss our babies for me. Your loving husband, Earl.

Vivian tucked the letter in with the rest without showing her in-laws. She'd gotten the mail that afternoon, so they didn't know she'd had a letter. She would have shown it to them if she thought it would bring comfort, but Mary cried at least once a day and often three or four times. Will forced himself to smile and laugh with the children, but between Earl's death and Mary's stroke, he seemed to be barely getting by. Vivian worried about both of her in-laws. And Sally. Carol and Lottie, so far, appeared untouched by their father's death, but Sally mourned him daily.

Of course EJ had no idea what had happened. Regardless, he fussed more than the girls had done as babies, and Vivian guessed he sensed her grief and weariness.

With Mary ill and confined to bed or the rocking chair, Carol and Lottie would have been impossible to corral, except that Vivian's mother was coming out to the farm every day to help care for Mary and for the children. Every morning, Vivian figured her mother wouldn't show up again—but then she did. Mum also knew things that surprised Vivian. How to pluck a chicken. How to milk a cow. How to make cottage cheese. All chores she'd never seen her mother do before.

Mum also soothed EJ when he was colicky, treated Lottie's earache, and talked Carol into eating her beans.

While Vivian was a little girl in London, Mum had hired a nanny and a maid. Later, in the US, Vivian realized that Daddy's income probably didn't cover it. Mum didn't work but had money of her own, undoubtedly from the estate of her first husband. Somewhere along the line Mum had learned how to care for children and do all sorts of other things too.

Mary improved in starts and stops, and gradually her right side improved enough that she could get around the house and even help with simple chores such as folding laundry and supervising the children and rocking EJ, holding him in her good arm.

But Vivian's stress, even with the help she had, was hard to manage.

One Wednesday in early May, at lunchtime, Vivian felt more overwhelmed than usual. Mum had a doctor's appointment and couldn't help that day. Mary said to Vivian, "Go to your knitting circle."

"No," Vivian said. "The children are too much."

"Will is going to watch the children," Mary said. "It was his idea that you go. We'll keep EJ too."

So Vivian reluctantly drove into town, but before she reached the church, she turned in to the Railroad District and stopped at her mother's house. Before she could climb out of the pickup, Mum came out onto the porch and then hurried down the stairs. "Vivian?" she called out. "Is everything okay?"

"Yes." Vivian lowered herself from the truck. "I'm going to the knitting circle. Would you come with me? Will you have time before your appointment?"

Without hesitating, Mum said, "Yes."

After they arrived and were situated, Martha read a devotional about women in the Bible who worked in the textile business, focusing on Lydia, who was a merchant, and Tabitha, who was a seamstress. "Clothing people is an honorable profession, and what all of you have done throughout this war is admirable. We've had thirty consistent knitters since just after Pearl Harbor. As a group, we've produced nearly two thousand items. Thank you." Martha exhaled. "Sadly, today we have some new patterns—toe covers and stump covers."

Vivian did her best to swallow a sob. Why couldn't Earl have been badly injured instead of killed? If only he'd come home, she would have gratefully cared for him the rest of his life. Gladly. Not that she didn't feel sympathy for all the sailors and soldiers who had lost limbs. She did. And she felt happy for their families, that their loved one would return. She just wished her family was one of them.

After Martha finished her presentation, Vivian went up to the table and chose a leg stump pattern while Mum chose a pattern for socks. Martha asked Vivian how she was doing. "All right," Vivian answered.

"How is Mary?"

"Better," Vivian said. "Thankfully."

Other women approached Vivian to ask how she was. But soon the conversations quieted. Women who were usually loud and laughed a lot spoke in hushed voices. With each passing moment, Vivian felt more ill at ease. The knitting circle had been such a place of comfort and support in the past, but then she was doing her bit for the war effort, all the time thinking about Earl. Now she'd done far more than her bit—she'd lost her husband. A half hour before the knitting circle ended, Vivian whispered to Mum that she was ready to go.

"All right." Mum put her project in her bag and then stood. She stepped to the front of the room. Vivian heard her say, "We've had a lovely time. Thank you."

Martha reached for Mum's hand and softly said, "Vivian is in our prayers."

As Vivian drove the pickup to Mum's, she fought her tears. She felt despondent, full of intense grief. She still couldn't imagine life without Earl. "I feel so empty, as if a whole chunk of my mind, heart, and body are missing. And as if everyone can tell. I'm a war widow. An uncomfortable reminder of what's happening."

"It's because people care," Mum said. "They hurt for you. They've been watching you since we moved to town. You and Earl were such a striking couple, so obviously in love. People are mourning with you. But with a tragedy of this magnitude, sometimes they don't know what to say."

Vivian hadn't thought of it that way. She shifted into first as she turned onto Mum's street. "What was it like for you after Daisy's dad passed away?"

"In time, I managed to persevere, as you will too."

Vivian choked on the words, "But how?"

When her mother didn't answer, Vivian stole a glance at her. Mum stared straight ahead.

Vivian swallowed down her tears. "I'm sorry," Vivian said.

Mum turned her head. "Don't be," she said gently. "I know I've never talked much about Luc with you, and I regret that now."

"Why?"

"Why didn't I talk about him?"

Vivian nodded.

"I didn't want it to seem I was disloyal to your father, who is a fine man." Mum folded her hands in her lap. "It really is possible to love again, to deeply love two very different men."

Vivian squeezed the steering wheel. She couldn't even imagine loving someone else.

"How did I carry on?" Mum said. "To be honest, I cried for the first two months and probably wouldn't have gotten out of bed if it wasn't for Daisy. She needed me. She forced me to keep living. Plus, she was so full of life, so full of ideas, and so full of drama. So different from me—but she was exactly what I needed."

Mum sighed. "Luc was a lot like Daisy. Blond hair and dark eyes. Lithe and athletic. When I first met him, I was smitten. But I knew my place. I was British and Protestant, and his secretary. I was from a poor family, although I'd had a good education and wealthy relatives who looked out for me. He was from a very wealthy French family and Catholic. When he seemed interested in me, I didn't believe it was genuine. But it was. I wasn't what his family envisioned for him, but they were kind and then even warm after Daisy was born. Luc was emotional, and sometimes moody, but he taught me to acknowledge and even share my own feelings. On the other hand, your dad has always been so—so optimistic. So happy."

Vivian hung on her mother's every word as they neared the house. Her mother had never shared so much, and Vivian was hungry to know more about this woman who had given birth to her and raised her.

"I haven't always been able to share my own feelings as much. I first met your father in Hyde Park. Daisy and I were there, feeding the ducks, and she became concerned with one that appeared injured. She leaped into the pond after it, and your father jumped in after her." She smiled at the memory. "No one in my family nor Luc's were thrilled when I decided to marry him." She stared down at the engagement ring and wedding band on her finger. "I had been madly, head over heels in love with Luc. On the other hand, I was older when I fell in love with your father—and sadder. But I loved—love—your father. He's been good to me, to us."

Vivian parked the truck and then reached over and put her right hand on top of her mother's hand. "Thank you for being good to me," Vivian said. "I can't imagine the last months without you."

"Honestly, it's been helpful for me to be needed again. I don't have as much time to worry about Daisy." Mum flipped her hands over and clasped and squeezed Vivian's. "You were always so independent, so capable, from the very beginning. You took after your father in that way. The can-do American."

"I take after you more than I realized," Vivian said. "Maybe more than you realize too."

Vivian felt numb all through the summer. In early September, Sally started first grade, which was a good distraction. Vivian's firstborn began to show glimmers of her old happy self.

Soon after that, Mum stopped coming every day, tapering off to three days a week and then two. Vivian understood. It was a lot for Mum to drive out to the farm and work so hard. She'd lost weight and looked gaunt. Daddy often came on Saturdays when he was in town to help Will with the farming.

In April, Mary had a massive stroke and died a day later. The family had another funeral, but this time with a body to bury. The pain of losing Earl and now Mary nearly crushed Vivian. Will remained stoic, throwing himself into the hard, physical labor of *running the farm, but he was clearly a broken man. Her grandmother's death set Sally back again for a couple of months. EJ was now just over a year old and walking and babbling away. Carol and Lottie mourned their grandmother but hardly spoke of their father. Children were resilient. She wished she could be more like them.*

In June, Vivian read in the paper that the Allies had finally arrived in France. D-Day. Three days later, the 2nd Armored Division landed on Omaha Beach. It was nearly another year until the war in Europe ended, and then another three months until Japan surrendered. When Vivian went into town, the streets around the depot were filled with soldiers and sailors, returning home. Her heart seared with loneliness.

Life went on. She never went to the knitting circle anymore, even though it continued. Service people still needed warm clothes. The calendar flipped to 1946. Vivian helped Will, who was feeling his age, more and more with the farming. Every month she hoped they'd bring in enough money to hire someone to help, but they never did. By June, when Sally was home all day from school and able to watch the younger children, Vivian worked the farm with Will for hours each day.

One afternoon while Will went into town for supplies, Vivian worked on digging a fence post hole. She watched the mailman stop his car and put a parcel on top of their box. Vivian decided to take a break, collect the mail, and check on the children.

When she reached the house with the parcel, the three younger children were still napping and Sally was reading. Vivian put the parcel, which was the size of a five-pound bag of sugar, on the table.

"Who is it from?" Sally asked.

"I'm not sure," Vivian said. It didn't have a return address, but the postage was British. Daisy? She tried not to get her hopes up. After cutting the twine with a knife, she opened the parcel. Inside was a copy of the Book of Common Prayer, *a photograph of Daisy and Vivian taken on Daisy's wedding day, a christening gown, a single knitting needle, and pieces of a vase wrapped in paper, which had apparently broken on the trip. Underneath the items was a letter from Adam Chapman Martin. He wrote that he was Noel Chapman's nephew and the current owner of the family's Berkshire manor, and had been since 1942. He'd found a box of things in what had been Daisy Dumont Chapman's room, with instructions to mail them to Vivian if Daisy didn't return after the war ended.*

I waited more than a year. I can only assume she's deceased. She seems to have disappeared in

August of 1942. I have no idea where she went, nor does anyone I've contacted. Her apartment in London was destroyed by that time. Please forgive me for being the bearer of sad but incomplete news. Sincerely yours, Adam Chapman Martin

Sally appeared at Vivian's side. "Who are these things from?"

"A man who lives in England."

"A book, broken glass..." Sally picked up the christening gown. "What's this?"

"A gown babies are baptized in." She and Daisy had been baptized in it. Vivian threw away the broken vase, which she remembered had belonged to their maternal grandmother whom she had never met, and put the picture between two pages of the Book of Common Prayer *to keep it from getting bent. She put everything in the box and then placed the box in her bottom bureau drawer. When she returned to the living room, Sally was back on the sofa reading. The little ones would sleep for a while longer.*

Vivian fought off her tears, not wanting to alarm Sally. "I'll be back out by the barn. Yell if you need me."

It wasn't until she reached the fence that Vivian let her tears flow. She brushed at them with her gloves, likely tracking gritty dirt across her cheeks. She took

off one glove and swiped at the mud with her bare fingers, probably only making it worse. Daisy was dead. If she wasn't, she would have written. Vivian had known that all along, but she couldn't deny it any longer. She'd need to tell Mum what she'd received. She hoped it wouldn't send her into another depression.

With her heart heavy, she put the gloves back on and thrust the posthole digger into the ground. She pulled it out and released the soil into a pile. And then did it again. And again. A vehicle turned up the drive. Will was home. She swiped at her tears again, this time with her sleeve.

"Vivian?" It was a voice she didn't recognize.

Her pulse raced. A soldier in uniform came toward her. Her heart kicked against her chest. It wasn't Earl. It would never be Earl. The man wasn't as tall or as broad shouldered. But he had a kind smile and caring brown eyes.

"I'm Ted. I served with Earl." He held up a packet of letters in one hand, and in the other, a ball of yarn and what looked like a scarf still attached to a knitting needle. "He asked if anything happened to him that I'd deliver these to you in person."

CHAPTER EIGHTEEN

*A*ll the next day, Debbie thought about Vivian as she waited on tables, made drinks, and delivered food. Several times she realized that Janet had repeated her name before Debbie heard her.

About an hour before closing time, Janet started frosting the cookies for the dance. When the last customer left, Debbie joined her. As she spread pink frosting on cookie after cookie, Debbie told Janet about what she'd learned the evening before. "Ted *did* bring the knitting project from Earl, according to Vivian's diary," she said, "just as Sally remembered."

"But why would Earl have had a knitting project in the first place?" Janet asked. "And why would Ted carry it from Tunisia to wherever he served next all the way to Dennison, Ohio?"

"Because he was like a brother to Earl." Debbie picked up another cookie. "Because he promised Earl he would."

After they made good progress on the cookies and Janet left, Debbie texted Sally. I HAVE MORE QUESTIONS FOR YOU. IS IT ALL RIGHT IF I COME BY?

She waited a few minutes without an answer and decided to head home. But then Sally texted her back. SURE. COME ON DOWN TO MY ROOM.

When Debbie knocked on Sally's door, she called out, "It's unlocked."

Debbie opened the door.

Sally stood in her kitchenette. "I'm making tea. Would you like a cup?"

"Yes," Debbie said. "Thank you."

"We always had tea after school with Grannie Olson when we lived with her. It's a tradition that I've tried to keep after all these years."

"Did your mother have tea in the afternoon?"

"Oh, she'd have a cup now and then, but nothing formal. She tried her best to be an American." Sally poured milk into each of two blue mugs and then poured the tea. She handed Debbie one of the mugs.

After they settled down in the little living room, Debbie said, "I found information in your mother's things about Ted bringing the knitting project."

Sally smiled wryly. "Now do you believe me?"

"Yes." Although there was no proof the ring had been in the ball of yarn Ted gave Vivian. She could have gotten the ring somewhere else and wrapped it in the ball of yarn later. "He arrived the day the package came from Daisy, just like you said." Debbie took a sip of tea and then speculated, "So let's say the ring belonged to Daisy but arrived in the middle of a ball of yarn that Ted brought that had been in your father's possession. How did your father get the ball of yarn?"

"Do we know for sure the ring belonged to Daisy? Because that would prove it's mine, that it came through my mother's family."

Debbie told her about the engagement ring Noel Chapman gave Daisy.

"Okay," Sally said thoughtfully. "It could be a coincidence. And it doesn't explain how my father got it and gave it to Ted for my mother. But however it happened, the ring belongs to me."

Debbie took another sip of tea. She was nearly sure the ring had been Daisy's, but Sally was right. She only had a blurry image and a description that matched the ring in the ball of yarn. It could be a coincidence. There was also no evidence of how Earl—or Ted—had obtained it. "Your mother mentioned a *Book of Common Prayer* that arrived with Daisy's things. Do you know what happened to it?"

"I think Lottie has it. Or at least she did." Sally took her phone from the pocket of her sweater. "I'll ask her."

After Sally finished sending the text, Debbie asked, "Did you see the ring the day Ted arrived?"

"No. I did see the yarn though. I think it was sometime later that Mama found the ring—I'm not sure if it was a few weeks or even a few months. I didn't get the idea that Ted knew it was there when he brought it."

"But you think your father knew the ring was in the ball of yarn?"

"Of course. He sent it to her."

Debbie wasn't so sure. It made sense that Sally believed that as a child—but the evidence wasn't there to support that Earl knew. Of course, there wasn't any evidence that he didn't, either. Or Ted, for that matter. But if there wasn't something valuable in the ball of yarn, why would he have asked Ted to make sure he took it to Vivian?

"Why did your mother keep the ring in the middle of the ball of yarn, especially when it seemed she knew it was valuable?" She'd asked this on a previous visit, but maybe Sally remembered something more now.

"Because she was sentimental," Sally said. "Daddy had put it in that ball of yarn for her because, first of all, he probably thought she'd get a kick out of the knitting project and, second of all, because it was a safe place for the ring. I'm thinking someone in Africa must have given both to him. Or perhaps he bartered for them. Anyway, Mama wanted to keep everything together in one place."

Perhaps Vivian had kept the ring as a kind of insurance policy. A valuable she could sell if times ever warranted it.

Sally's phone rang. She held it up. "It's Brant."

"Go ahead and answer it." Debbie smiled.

Sally accepted the call and held the phone to her ear. "Hello, Brant."

He spoke loudly enough that Debbie could clearly hear him. "Mom," he said, "I'm going to do it. I'm going to propose to Cassie. Did you get that ring?"

Sally stood. "I'm so glad to hear that you're going to propose." She walked down her little hall. "That's great. When?"

Debbie couldn't hear Brant's response.

Sally listened for a minute or two and said, "Debbie's here." There was another pause. "You know, Greg's girlfriend." There was a longer pause and then, "I'll call you back in a little bit. I love you. Bye." Then Sally turned toward Debbie. "That was Brant. He's planning on proposing to his girlfriend."

"Oh, that's wonderful." Debbie didn't let on that she'd heard that part of the conversation. "When?"

"Probably by the end of the month." As Sally sat, her phone dinged. She glanced down. "It's Lottie. She's going to drive down tomorrow." Sally raised her head. "Lottie said she'll bring the prayer book."

As Debbie changed into a flared dress for dancing class, she thought about Sally. Was Brant asking for Vivian's ring to propose to his girlfriend? It almost had to be, rather than some other ring Sally had. Had Sally taken the ring all those years ago and planted it back in the box so Greg would find it? And then she could claim it as rightfully hers and give it to Brant? It seemed as plausible an explanation as Katherine planting the ring in the box and subsequently claiming a right to it.

And yet, why go to all this trouble? Greg had never seen the ring before, nor had Paulette. So if Brant's fiancée turned up wearing it, they'd be none the wiser.

Later at dance class, Meg was delighted to see Debbie. "It was so fun to show you the old Johnston place yesterday," she gushed. Then she turned to Greg and said, "I'm certain I knew you when you were a boy. It's so nice to see you again now."

"Likewise," Greg said. "It's always a pleasure to meet people who knew my grandmother."

Meg pressed her hands together as if she were praying. "She was such a good person. Really, the best."

"I think so too," Greg said.

Meg smiled, stepped out into the middle of the room, and then called out, "Are you ready to dance tonight? It's our last lesson before Friday night's fun!"

Jeff started the music, and Meg began calling out, "Rock step…"

Overall, they did better than at the previous lessons, except that this time Greg seemed preoccupied and distant. Debbie didn't tell him about the beginning of the conversation she'd overheard at Sally's, but on the way home she did ask him about her. "How is she doing financially? Any problems?"

"I can't imagine she's doing well. Dan fought one cancer after another for thirty years. He retired early. Sally cared for him. They lived in Brant's basement apartment for the last few years. I imagine they wiped out their savings and retirement investments. She probably has a pension from Dan's work. Hopefully it's enough to cover Good Shepherd—except I know it's pretty expensive." Greg shrugged. "I'm only speculating. But unless Dan's family had money I never heard about, I don't imagine Sally has a lot."

"What about Brant?"

"I think he does okay. He has his own automotive garage. His first marriage didn't end well, but they didn't have kids. He's been single for the last ten years. I would think he's saved quite a bit, though who knows?" Greg stopped in front of Debbie's house. "Why do you ask?"

"I'm not saying Sally had the ring and then planted it in the box on your porch—or more likely Brant would have—but if they had something to do with it, what would the motivation be? Obviously, if Sally already had the ring, it would be simple for her to claim ownership of it and be able to use it legitimately, in public. I mean, in front of the family."

"To wear it?"

"Perhaps," Debbie said. "But maybe to give it away. Or to sell it if she's short on funds to finance her stay at Good Shepherd."

"I hate to think of Sally in need of money," Greg said. "If she is, I hope she would let us know."

Debbie thought of Sally shutting down after she found out her father was dead and then after her grandmother had died too. Had she hit a wall after Dan passed away? Was Sally not doing as well emotionally as she seemed?

When Greg pulled up in front of Debbie's house, she said, "You don't need to walk me up to the porch. I know it's a school night and you need to get home to the boys."

He groaned. "This is my least favorite part of my life."

She tilted her head. "What is?"

"Telling you goodbye. Driving away."

"Aw," she said. "That's so sweet."

He opened his door. "I won't *not* walk you up to your porch. But then I do need to go. Jaxon didn't do so well on his biology test. He's cramming before he retakes it in the morning. I told him I'd help him study." Greg jumped down, closed his door, and then jogged around to Debbie's door. He opened it and said, "Watch out. There's a little river running along the curb."

"I hope this doesn't all refreeze," Debbie said. "We might be ice skating instead of dancing on Friday."

Greg took Debbie's hand as they reached the sidewalk and took two steps. Somehow Debbie followed his lead without any notice. Then he rocked back, and she followed again. Finally, he twirled her around, but the bulk of her coat made dancing difficult, and she stumbled backward. "I think we've got it." He laughed as he caught her. "We'll be fine Friday night."

She laughed too and then hurried up to the porch, dragging Greg along. She wrapped her arms around him, and he squeezed her tight in what she thought would be a quick hug, considering how distracted he'd seemed earlier. Instead, he held her for a long moment and brushed his lips against her forehead. "I wish I could stay," he said.

"So do I," she answered. "But a biology exam calls."

He laughed. "I'll talk to you in the morning."

"I can't wait."

Greg kissed her and then bounded down the stairs. Debbie watched until his pickup pulled away from the curb and turned left at the corner. He didn't wave like he usually did.

After changing into jeans and a sweatshirt, Debbie sat at the table. Before she went through more of Vivian's letters and diaries, she checked her email. *Voilà!* The woman in France had emailed her back.

> *Hello, Debbie!*
>
> *I received your email and photos. I have been researching female spies during World War II and those who used knitting in their espionage for the last several years. I'll share a little of what I know.*
>
> *There was a network of female spies in France during World War II. They arrived from England, parachuting into the French countryside from 1942 to 1944. All had some sort of connection to France and could pass as French. They did*

all sorts of things, from blowing up trains to passing on intelligence to the French underground to working as radio operators. Some knitted intelligence into scarves and sweaters, including information about German troop movement, train schedules, and the status of spies. Some spies knotted Morse code messages into the yarn and then knitted the yarn into a garment. Once the "message" was delivered, the piece was unraveled, and the message deciphered. Others knit the Morse code message into the garment, using sequences of knit or purl. Others didn't use Morse code at all but relied on other established codes to send messages. Because knitting is binary, it lends itself to coding. A knitting pattern looks similar to code in the first place.

As far as the scarf, it appears there may be a Morse code message in it, but I can't make it out. Perhaps it's the quality of the photographs or maybe the wool has deteriorated through the years. Or perhaps you or someone else can make out the message. Obviously, the message would mean something to the person who was intended to receive the ball of yarn, needles, and scarf. I hope that person did, in fact, receive it and knew to decipher the message.

If you have the name of the person who may have sent the knitting project, I would be willing to do some research for you. If you have a possible code name, that would be helpful too.

Sincerely,

Marietta Aubert

"Wow." Debbie sent Marietta a reply, first thanking her for her information and then giving her background information on Daisy Dumont Chapman.

She grew up in London but spent summers in France with her father's family, who owned a textile company— Dumont Textiles—and had homes in Paris and Normandy. Daisy was fluent in French. Her husband was killed in the Battle of Singapore, and she was determined to do what she could for the war effort. Her last letters to her sister and mother, who both lived in Dennison, Ohio, were dated April 1942. I haven't found any information about Daisy after that. I have no idea what her code name would have been if she worked as a spy. Thank you for any information you can give me.

After Debbie hit Send, she took the scarf out of the bag. The odd pattern had meaning. But what? She ran her fingers over the stitches and then did some research on Morse code. Some of the stitches were frayed, and some had disintegrated and left holes. Debbie needed help from someone who knew Morse code. It could take her forever.

She put the scarf back in the bag. Had Daisy parachuted into France? That would have taken a fair amount of training. But if she was in France, there was no way she could have given the scarf to Earl. He never made it to France. Debbie had more unanswered questions than ever. She stood. It was too late to search for any more answers tonight. And she wouldn't have much time tomorrow.

Hopefully Marietta Aubert could find the answers that neither Debbie nor Janet had been able to locate.

Debbie woke at four a.m., tossing and turning. Then she checked her email. She hadn't expected a response from Marietta this soon—and she was correct in her expectation. There wasn't one. She decided to get up for the day. She'd have an extra hour—and she knew exactly how she wanted to spend it. Going through Vivian's boxes.

After making a cup of coffee and cinching her robe against the chilly morning, Debbie sat down at the dining room table. She had two objectives: to go through the rest of the photos and to go through Earl's letters again to see if she'd missed anything now that she knew more of the story. First, she looked through the remaining stack of photos. There were a few of two boys, Greg and Brant. Greg was taller although Brant was older. Both had thousand-watt smiles and looked as if they were having the time of their lives. The boys posed outside in all the photos—on the porch, next to the chicken coop with hammers, and in front of the barn with Vivian, who wore a dress with an apron over it and sturdy shoes. Debbie guessed Vivian was around seventy in the photo—and still as beautiful as when she was a young woman.

Next were several photos of a thin and ill Vivian with Sally, Carol, Lottie, EJ, and Brenda. Five of the seven children must have gathered together to be with her before she died.

Near the bottom of the pile was a photo of a young woman with Vivian in the house. They sat side by side on the sofa. Vivian appeared gaunt and had a blanket over her lap. The young woman held a tray in her hands.

Debbie stared at the photo. The young woman looked familiar. Very familiar.

Meg? Had she actually helped care for Vivian in the last months of her life? If so, why hadn't Sally or Meg told Debbie that? Debbie snapped a picture of the photo with her phone, composed a text to Sally, and then remembered what time it was. Too early to send a text.

She flipped quickly through the rest of the photos. None stood out, either as clues to the mystery or for inclusion in Kim's exhibit.

Debbie turned her attention to Earl's letters. She thumbed through them, finding the ones he sent from North Africa. She'd already read these once before. Now she thought it wouldn't hurt to scan through them again. The third one said:

> There are so many things I can't tell you, of course, one being of a very pleasant surprise that resulted in a gift for you. I'll tell you all about it when I come home. You won't need to remind me. Amazing to have some good happen among all the bad.

When Debbie read the letter the first time, she'd thought it odd. Now she wondered if Earl had met Daisy. But what would Daisy be doing in Morocco or Algeria? It was one thing to think of her parachuting into Normandy—but how would she have gotten to North Africa? Debbie searched *Allied spies in North Africa* on her laptop. Josephine Baker, an American-French jazz singer, spied for the

Allies in Morocco and worked with a network of other Allied spies—so there were definitely female operatives.

What about the yarn? Daisy could have brought it with her. Or surely sheep were raised in North Africa. She looked that up too and found a breed native to the area that gave "carpet-grade" wool.

What about the idea of a code knitted into a garment? Daisy had told Vivian about the woman in Belgium during World War I who included code in her knitting. It had made enough of an impression for Vivian to knit Morse code into Earl's scarf. It seemed logical Daisy knew about espionage work being done this way.

And Daisy had the perfect excuse to be in Algeria—her family textile business. No doubt her grandfather had worked out a deal with the Vichy government to open an office there. Could spying for the Allies right under the noses of the Vichy regime have been part of her grandfather's plan?

Daisy could pass as French. If she used an alias, no one would suspect her of being British. She was fluent in French, English, Morse code, maybe other codes, and could knit. Plus, she was vivacious, dramatic, and fearless. She was also used to hobnobbing with the elite and moving between cultures. Daisy Chapman would have made a perfect spy.

But why would Daisy have sent the ring to Vivian instead of keeping it for herself to barter for necessities if needed? Would she give it to Vivian instead of giving it back to the Dumont family, if in fact it had come from them? Was she in danger in Algeria? Perhaps someone had outed her as a spy. Or perhaps she feared what the Allies might do to her because of her family's connections, even if they were subversive, to the government of Vichy France.

From what Debbie had uncovered of Daisy so far, her guess was that Daisy would have chosen to send the ring to Vivian instead of keeping it or returning it.

What happened to Daisy after the spring of 1943? Was she killed in North Africa? Or did she manage to return to France? France wasn't free. D-Day was still over fourteen months away. Paris wouldn't be liberated until August of 1944. A network of spies, including women, were working in France to make way for the D-Day invasion. That gave Daisy more than a year to be part of the resistance in France.

If she'd parachuted into France, sent coded messages via knitted garments, and helped with D-Day and forcing the Nazis out of Normandy, surely she wouldn't stop until all of France was free. Or she was dead.

If Earl did somehow see Daisy in North Africa, he couldn't write to Vivian about it at the time. If the letter fell into the wrong hands, Daisy's cover would be blown.

If Daisy gave Earl the scarf and the ball of yarn, did she tell him about the ring inside? Did she tell him about the Morse code message knitted into the scarf? Surely, considering he had a scarf with a message of its own, he would have deciphered the message. If not, would Vivian have known to look for it? Debbie thought of Earl's scarf again. Of course Vivian would have realized Daisy had knitted a message into the scarf.

Debbie shivered. She left the letter from Earl on the table and then peered down into the box. Had she missed anything? She ran her hand along the bottom. Her finger brushed up against something. Debbie shone her phone flashlight into the box. There was a white piece of paper sticking out of the overlaps in the bottom of the box. She pulled it out. It was a folded typed note on a sheet of paper with a Crane crest watermark on the bottom. Debbie remembered that sort of paper from her childhood. The signature read *Vivian Johnston (Mama)*. It was dated September 13, 1992, and simply read, *I want Sally to have the ring in my bottom drawer. I've never had it appraised, but I'm certain it's valuable, more than I've ever let on.*

Was the note legitimately typed and signed by Vivian? Or had someone—it would have to be Sally or perhaps Brant—typed it recently and forged Vivian's signature? Perhaps Kim could help Debbie determine when the note had been composed.

She headed upstairs to shower.

Debbie thought about texting Greg to tell him about what she had found, but he was getting two teenagers out the door and to school. She didn't want to intrude. And he hadn't called her in the mornings the last couple of days. It had been a weird week with Greg. One day, like Sunday, he was overly attentive. Other days, like at their dance class last night, he seemed distracted, sometimes even distant. She tried not to read too much into it. He was busy with the boys and the new contracting project he was working on.

At seven, a minute after she flipped the sign to open the café, Kim stepped through the door.

"You're here early."

"I know. That's why I need coffee." Kim glanced at the pastry tray. "And how about one of Janet's cinnamon rolls too?"

"You've got it." As Debbie poured the coffee in a to-go cup, she asked Kim how Barry was doing. "Much better. He's been diagnosed with arrhythmia. He started on medication, although he may need to have a device implanted. The doctor is going to give the medication a try and then decide what to do next."

Debbie put the coffee on the counter. "Will he be able to dance tomorrow?"

"The doctor said one or two dances but not to overdo it." Kim smiled. "We're both relieved to know what's going on."

"It's the unknown that's always the hardest." Debbie put the cinnamon roll in a box. "I have a note to show you from Vivian's boxes. I'm hoping you can help verify the age of it."

"Oh?"

"I'll go get it." Debbie had put the note in an envelope and in her purse.

After she handed it to Kim, she said, "Do you think this was written in the early 1990s or recently?"

Kim held the piece of paper up to the light. "Well, it seems the paper is genuinely from several decades ago. And it appears to have been typed on an old typewriter, not printed from a computer. Of course someone could have had some old paper and an old typewriter around. But the ink is faded." She set the paper on the counter. "I'll contact a friend of mine that works with paper and ink. Do you mind if I take it for today? I'll take good care of it."

"I know you will," Debbie said. "Let me know what you find out."

After Kim left, Debbie sent Sally the photo of the picture of Vivian with the young woman. A few minutes later, Sally replied, THAT'S MEG SINCLAIR WITH MAMA.

Debbie asked, DID MEG HELP TAKE CARE OF YOUR MOTHER REGULARLY?

Oh, Debbie, I'd forgotten that! Yes, she'd fill in when Paulette, EJ, or I couldn't be there. It was a blessing that she was willing to be one of Mama's caretakers. She spent multiple days with Mama when we couldn't.

Debbie stared at her phone. She'd already known Meg was interested in knitting. Was it possible that she taken the ball of yarn and scarf? Meg made it sound as if Sally and EJ took care of Vivian. Yet, Sally was saying Meg cared for her too.

Meg had the opportunity by being alone in the house with Vivian. But did she have the motivation? Debbie had no way of knowing if Meg knew there was a ring in the middle of the ball of yarn. She did know Meg was interested, by that time, in knitting and yarn. Perhaps she wanted a memento from Vivian but didn't know about the ring. Or perhaps she was fascinated with the odd yarn and scarf and the unusual needles. Debbie had no way of knowing any of that. But how would Meg have known that Paulette was going to put the boxes on Greg's porch the day of the snowstorm? And even if she did, what would have made her want to get rid of the yarn and scarf, let alone the ring, now?

Debbie obviously had more questions than answers.

CHAPTER NINETEEN

Before Debbie left the café, she texted Greg. A WOMAN IN FRANCE WHO HAS DONE RESEARCH ON FEMALE SPIES DURING WORLD WAR II THINKS THAT MORSE CODE WAS KNITTED INTO THE SCARF. DO YOU KNOW ANYONE WHO KNOWS MORSE CODE? IT WOULD TAKE ME A WHILE TO FIGURE IT OUT.

When Greg didn't return her text, Debbie headed home to get something to eat and to change her clothes before going back to the depot to help set up for the dance. As she reached the house, her phone dinged. It was Greg. SORRY I DIDN'T CALL THIS MORNING. I HAD AN OUT-OF-TOWN MEETING AND LEFT EARLY. I KNOW MORSE CODE, OR AT LEAST I USED TO. BRING THE SCARF TO THE DEPOT THIS EVENING, AND I'LL SEE WHAT I CAN FIGURE OUT.

Debbie replied, I WILL. I ALSO FOUND A NOTE IN YOUR GRAND-MOTHER'S THINGS LAST NIGHT TO SHOW YOU.

Greg didn't text back. Five minutes later, she was out the door and walking toward the depot. Her phone buzzed. It was a number she didn't recognize. Not at all. It started with a country code—+33. Debbie slowed her pace as she accepted the call. "This is Debbie Albright."

"Debbie, this is Marietta, calling from France. I found some information for you." She articulated each syllable, speaking English extremely well. "I saw your number at the bottom of your email and thought I'd call. Do you have a moment?"

"Yes, yes, of course."

"I've gone through the information I have about female spies in France. There were two who served in Algeria from 1942 to 1943 and then moved on to France in 1943 before D-Day," Marietta said. "There's not much information about the women who spied in Algeria, but there's quite a bit available, both from the British and from our government about female spies in France, including real names, code names, dates of when they arrived, what happened to them, if they made it out before the end of the war, if they were captured by the Germans, and if they were killed. There are a few spies who disappeared whose identities have never been confirmed, including one who was in Algeria."

"What was the woman's name?"

"Collette Laurent."

Debbie crossed the railroad tracks. "What makes you think that it could be Daisy?"

"Laurent was Daisy's paternal grandmother's family name," Marietta replied. "Collette was listed as a niece of Andre Dumont's when she worked for Dumont Textiles in Algeria. She parachuted into France in July of 1943."

"What was her code name?"

"Kitty Ball. Does the name mean anything to you?"

Debbie reached the depot and leaned against the brick wall to the left of the entrance. "No...except Kitty sounds a little like knitting. And ball could be a ball of yarn. What information is there about Kitty Ball?"

"British records show she started training with the War Office to work as a spy in the spring of 1942. While in France she passed knitted fabric containing intelligence to radio operators, about German troop movements mostly. She had access to German officers during part of her time in France. She also met other spies who parachuted into France and accompanied some to Paris, where it seems she had connections with German officers too. She was involved in bombing railroad tracks and power lines before D-Day, essentially helping to cut the Germans in Normandy off from the rest of France. Although she worked throughout Normandy, she lived on the peninsula."

"The Cotentin Peninsula?"

"*Oui*. But by the middle of June, she disappeared. There was a forty-two percent fatality rate for Allied female spies in the country, so…"

Debbie gasped. "That's horrible."

"Yes, it was dangerous work. They were a forward unit and provided the groundwork for the Allied landing during D-Day and beyond. It wouldn't have happened without them. They were well trained before they ever landed in France. They knew the risks."

"Any speculation on what happened to Daisy, aka Kitty Ball?"

"Oui. Several women in the Dumont family—her grandmother, aunt, and a cousin—all worked for the resistance in France in both Normandy and then in Paris. Germans confiscated their Paris house and parts of the Normandy chateau, but the family was allowed to live in the servant quarters of both properties because the men in the family cooperated with the Nazis and made the fabrics Germany needed—silk for parachutes, wool for uniforms. That sort of thing. At first the Nazis trusted the Dumont family, but after D-Day it seems their suspicions grew to the point they turned against the family in early August of 1944. That information has come out in the last decade. The grandmother and aunt were murdered in Paris by the Nazis while the cousin was sent to Bergen-Belsen, where she died, most likely from typhus."

"But there's no record of what happened to Daisy Chapman?"

"No," Marietta said. "Some have speculated she was killed with her grandmother and aunt and her body disposed of, but there's no evidence she ever arrived in Paris. Most likely she died in Normandy that June."

"Why wouldn't the British have a record of Daisy working as a spy? She would have been recruited and trained. Surely she would have a file on record."

"I'm not sure," Marietta said. "She should have—but for some reason she doesn't. It seems she adopted the name Collette Laurent when she first went to work with the British."

"Any idea why she would do that?"

"She was a war widow. Her husband's family owned land and a country home and were quite wealthy. It would have been quite scandalous for her to go off to war—not ladylike behavior for someone of her standing," Marietta said. "Also, having the last name of Laurent identified her as French instead of British."

"What a tragedy."

"There are endless tragedies that came out of World War II." Marietta was silent for a moment, then asked, "Did you decipher the code in the scarf?"

"Not yet," Debbie said. "But I hope to this evening. I'll let you know what I find out."

"Thank you. Let me know what else you discover too."

Debbie stepped into the depot. Janet had already affixed the Valentine decorations made last Saturday to the walls of the lobby, giving it even more of an old-fashioned feel with the hearts, doilies, old cards, and lace. Greg was already there too, on a ladder hanging a spotlight. Jeff and Meg Sinclair stood below, giving directions. When Greg saw her, he gave her a wave but not his usual boisterous hello.

She waved and headed to the back of the lobby, where Janet stood by a stack of tables. "I'll help." She put her purse and the bag with the knitting project next to the door to the café.

As Debbie and Janet put up tables, Jeff and Meg gave Greg directions about how to direct the spotlight. After a few minutes, he had it right, and Meg said to Jeff, "I'm going to go tell Debbie goodbye, and then we should go."

Debbie gave Meg a smile as she approached.

Meg said, "We wanted a spotlight for the dance competition. Thank goodness Greg was here already. I didn't want Jeff to get up on the ladder." She paused a moment and then said, "I've been thinking so much about Vivian since our talk. I was so fond of her."

"I've been thinking about our talk too." Debbie and Janet flipped a table over, and then Debbie took a step around the table toward Meg. "Did Vivian ever mention her sister Daisy?"

"Not that I remember." Meg wrinkled her nose. "That was so long ago, but I think I would remember if she had a sister, and I don't. Why?"

"The scarf may have come from her sister after World War II. Did she talk about that period of her life with you?"

"No." Meg rubbed her arms. "Vivian was a joyful person and took great delight in her children and grandchildren, but there was also a sadness in her. One time I asked her about World War II, and she said she didn't make a habit of talking about what happened back then."

"I think a lot of people moved on after the war," Debbie said. "Soldiers. People on the home front. Some came around to talking about it when they were older. But Vivian had a lot of losses, more than some."

Meg nodded. "Well, see you tomorrow. We'll dance our hearts out and remember the good times—not the bad."

Debbie smiled. "See you tomorrow."

Jeff and Greg, who had been talking, told each other goodbye, and then Greg approached Debbie and Janet. "Any other ladder-climbing jobs that need to be done?"

"No," Debbie said. "But I do have that decoding job for you."

He grinned. "I brushed up—I learned it in Boy Scouts and taught Jaxon and Julian a few years ago. I'm ready to give it a go. If I get stuck, I can always refer to an online chart I found."

"I'll get it." Debbie came back with the bag, pulled out the knitting project, and then spread the scarf flat on the table.

Greg leaned over the table with a hand planted on either side of the scarf. Then he asked, "Do you have a pen and a piece of paper?"

"Yes." She retrieved those from her bag and handed them to Greg.

He wrote down two dots, a dash and a dot, three dots, two more dots, a dash and two dots, and one dot.

On a new line he wrote a dash and then three dots, a dot and a dash, and dot dash, dot, and dot with the number two at the end.

He continued on until the piece of paper was full. Then he began writing words next to the lines of dots.

inside
ball
use
for
children
remember
who
taught
you
to
knit

Greg glanced up at Debbie. "Who taught Grandma how to knit?"

"Daisy."

"So the ring wasn't from Grandpa?"

"I think this confirms the ring came via your grandfather and then Ted. But it originated with Daisy."

"But how did Grandpa get Daisy's ring?"

Debbie described the cryptic paragraph in one of Earl's letters to Vivian while he was in North Africa, most likely in Algeria. "There's speculation that Daisy lived in Algeria under the name Collette Laurent and worked for Dumont Textiles, while also working as a spy for the Allies. Then, it seems she went back to England and parachuted into France in 1943. Again, she worked as a spy, possibly with three of her female Dumont relatives."

"Did she survive the war?" Greg asked.

"There's no record that she did."

Greg frowned. "Poor Grandma. She lost so much."

After a moment of silence, Janet asked, "Does that bring you any closer to figuring out how the ring got inside the box on your porch?"

Greg glanced at Debbie, who answered, "No." She told them about the note she found in the bottom of the box. "Kim is consulting with a colleague about the legitimacy of the note. Hopefully it will help you figure out who the ring should go to now."

"Well, if the note is legitimate, then the ring goes to Sally. Daisy wanted it to help Vivian's children." Greg put his hands in the pockets of his jacket. "Sally needs financial help. It's probably not exactly what Daisy intended, but I'd say the timing is perfect."

After Greg left, Janet and Debbie spread the red cloths over the tables and then pulled up eight chairs to each one. Janet had made silhouettes of several couples swing dancing as centerpieces, so they put those in place too.

"Let's put the scrapbook display on this table." Janet pointed to one of the two closest to the café door. "That way people can look at them as they drink their beverages and eat their goodies."

Janet picked up a large black trifold panel and set it in the middle of the table, then opened it up all the way. She'd enlarged fifteen photos from the previous year's Valentine's Day Swing Dance. All were attached to the board with black, old-fashioned adhesive corners.

Debbie stepped closer. "How fun!" There was a photo of Barry and Kim dancing cheek to cheek. One of Janet and Ian clapping at the end of a song. One of Debbie and Greg. "Is that Meg and Jeff?" Debbie asked. Meg was holding the skirt of her dress and bowing slightly with her right hand held up above her head, her palm facing inward. Debbie leaned in. "Look at Meg's ring."

Janet stepped closer to the display board. "I hadn't noticed the ring on Meg's finger."

"Well, I have rings on my mind lately. Do you have a color photo of this picture? Or just black and white?"

"I have it in color. Kim gave me all of these." Janet took her phone from the pocket of her sweatshirt. "She shared her cloud storage with me from last year's dance. I'll pull it up."

Janet fiddled with her phone and handed it to Debbie, who zoomed in on the ring. "It looks like Daisy's ring—or one that's identical to it." A wave of nausea came over her. "Meg was so convincing that she'd never seen the old knitting project before." She turned to Janet. "What do you think I should do?"

"Someone needs to confront her, but talk to Greg and see how he wants to handle it. It's not like Meg is going to be arrested or anything—but still, if she took the knitting project and ring all those years ago, even though she was young, she should still be held accountable."

Debbie agreed. "She's most likely the one who put the knitting project in the box on Greg's porch." Debbie's phone buzzed with a text. "I'll ask his neighbors and see if anyone saw her pickup in the neighborhood that Saturday morning." She glanced down at her phone. "It's from Sally. Lottie and Katherine are at her place, and she invited me over." She raised her head. "Want to come with me?"

"Sure," Janet said. "But ask Sally if that's all right."

Debbie texted Sally who replied, ABSOLUTELY!

"I hope Lottie brought *The Book of Common Prayer*." She told Janet that Vivian had written about tucking the photo into the book.

Janet chuckled. "So the ring has been captured by the camera twice?"

"Three times, maybe. The engagement photo isn't very clear."

As they exited the depot, Janet said, "I'll drive," motioning to her car. After they were inside and their seat belts fastened, Janet said, "Is it my imagination or has Greg been acting strange lately?"

"What do you mean?"

"He's been kind of quiet." Janet backed out of the parking space. "Distracted."

Debbie could feel her countenance fall. "I've noticed that too. But he has a lot going on."

"I'll bet he does," Janet said.

After they reached Good Shepherd and headed inside, Debbie said, "They must be in Sally's room."

The door was cracked open, but Debbie knocked.

"Come on in," Sally called out.

As they entered the living room, Sally introduced Debbie and Janet to Lottie and then Janet to Katherine. Lottie wore an expensive-looking pantsuit, rings on both hands, gold bracelets on her wrists, and designer shoes. Katherine was dressed similarly. Sally wore a comfortable-looking velour sweatsuit.

After everyone had greeted each other, Lottie held up a book. "I brought our great-grandmother's *Book of Common Prayer*."

"Thank you," Debbie said. "In your mother's diary she wrote that she put a photograph of Daisy and her in the book."

Lottie held up a photograph. "I thought this might be what you were looking for."

"Now the big question is, does Daisy have a ring on her finger?" Debbie asked. She held her breath.

Lottie put on reading glasses and stared at the photo. "Aunt Daisy is wearing the ring that was in Mama's ball of yarn. I never noticed that before." Sally snatched the photo away from her sister.

"I remember the first time I saw the ring," Lottie said. "I was around eight and went snooping through Mama's drawers. I found the yarn. I knew not to unravel it from the scarf, so I stuck my fingers in, looking for the other end. Instead, I found the ring."

"And you came running into the living room with it on your thumb, yelling, 'Look what I found!'" Sally said. "Mama went white and took it away from you. Then she said, 'Children, your father sent this to me when he was in the war. It's old and worn, but I'm sentimental about it. Please do not go through my drawers again, Lottie. That goes for all of you.'" Sally grinned. "Or something like that."

"Of course I didn't pull the ring out very often," Lottie said, "but I did occasionally. It was so odd that she kept it in that ball of yarn."

"I have some information that might explain why she did." Debbie shared what she'd learned about the knitted piece, the ball of yarn, and Earl's letter to Vivian from when he was in North Africa. "It seems likely that at some point, Daisy and Earl met, most likely in Algeria."

Lottie put her hands to her face.

"What?" Sally asked.

Lottie's hands dropped to her chest. "Grandma Charlotte once said that she'd told Daddy to look for Daisy if he ended up in France. There was speculation that the Allied troops would cross the English Channel and end up in Normandy, earlier. Maybe even by the summer of 1943. That's not what happened, of course, and Daddy was sent to North Africa instead. She also told him that in one of Daisy's letters—it was written before Daisy's husband was killed—she said that her French grandfather had opened an office for his company in Algeria."

"You remember all that?" Sally asked.

"Of course. I was fascinated by anything Grannie told me. Life in London. Daisy. Mama when she was a little girl playing in Hyde Park." Lottie tapped her manicured fingers against her chin. "I can't remember what the business was."

"Dumont Textiles," Debbie said. So far, everything Lottie said confirmed what Debbie already knew. "Their headquarters was in Paris. Daisy's father, Luc, opened up a branch in London, which closed after he died. Then Daisy's grandfather, Andre, received permission from the Vichy Government to open a branch in Algeria in 1941."

Sally crossed her arms. "How do you know all of that?"

Debbie patted Janet's shoulder. "I had some help from Janet and also from a woman in France. She believes Daisy may have been a spy for the Allies, both in Algeria and then in France before and after D-Day."

Lottie nodded. "Grandma said she liked to pretend that Daisy and Daddy had seen and met each other before they died. They both loved Mama so much—she thought it only right that they would have met."

Debbie's eyes filled with tears, thinking about Vivian's heavenly reunion when she died. Her parents. Daisy. Earl. And Ted.

"Well." Katherine stood. "I owe all of you an apology. It seems, perhaps, the ring didn't come from the Johnston family after all."

"Perhaps?" Sally asked.

"We still don't know that Ted didn't take one similar. The Johnston ring could be the one Vivian ended up with."

Sally crossed her arms. "But why would Ted say it was from Earl, and why would it be in a ball of yarn?"

Katherine shrugged. Obviously, Katherine was determined to come up with a narrative about the Johnston ring, whether it was accurate or not.

Sally turned to Debbie. "Has Greg decided what to do with Mama's ring?"

"You should ask him," Debbie said, not revealing the existence of the typed note just yet. "Do you all plan to come to the dance tomorrow evening?"

Lottie's eyes sparkled. "We wouldn't miss it."

Once Debbie was home, she called Greg. He didn't answer, but a couple of minutes later he called back. "Sorry I missed your call. What's up?" He sounded distant again.

She filled him in about the photograph of Vivian and Daisy, who was wearing the ring, and what Lottie remembered about Charlotte giving Earl information about the Dumonts' business in Algiers.

"Wow," Greg said. "You've really put this puzzle together, haven't you?"

"Well, I hope we'll know if the note about Sally getting the ring is authentic or not by tomorrow."

"I hope so too. I'd like to have this all figured as soon as possible. I'd rather not be responsible for that ring any longer than I need to be. Not that it's in any danger in the safety deposit box." He paused a moment. "But we're not any closer to figuring out how the ring ended up on my porch, are we?"

"Actually," Debbie said. "It seems we are." She told him about Meg helping care for Vivian and the photograph of Meg from last year's dance.

"That's hard to believe," Greg said. "She's so nice. I'd never expect that of her."

"I know, right? But she had the opportunity."

"But did she have a motive? She didn't sell it. And why would she have worn it to the dance last year in public like that?"

"Maybe the motive wasn't to take the ring. Maybe she took the scarf and ball of yarn and then found the ring afterward."

"Why would anyone want to steal a ball of yarn and unfinished scarf?"

"That's what I'm trying to figure out too," Debbie said. "Think about what you'd like to do."

"Like, do you mean, confront her?"

"Yes," Debbie said. "It's your decision."

Greg groaned. "I'll think about it."

After Debbie and Greg told each other good night, she sat back down at the table, determined to get through the rest of Vivian's story.

CHAPTER TWENTY

Connor Farm, Dennison, Ohio
June 17, 1946

Vivian leaned against the posthole digger to steady herself as she stared at the soldier. He extended the packet of letters. Earl's letters. Finally, she said, "Come on down to the house," just as another vehicle door slammed shut, but closer. Will had parked by the barn.

Vivian straightened up. "Come meet Earl's father first."

Ted put the items into his rucksack and slung it over his shoulder. Vivian led the way to the barn as she called out, "Will!"

As she came around the side of the barn, she saw Will standing at the back of the truck bed with a bag of feed in his hands. Will turned his head. A look of shock passed over his face, and he staggered backward and stumbled. He dropped the bag and then tripped over it, landing with his left leg at an odd angle.

Will groaned as Vivian rushed to him, followed by Ted.

Will gasped, reached for his leg, and then said, "I thought you were Earl."

"I'm sorry, sir." Ted kneeled by Will's leg.

Will gasped again. "I'm afraid I broke it," he said to Vivian.

Vivian's voice quavered. "I'll take you down to Doc's office." She hoped the break wasn't bad—an injury at Will's age could leave him with long-term damage. "I'll see if a neighbor can stay with the kids."

"I have a car—that I'm borrowing." Ted stood. "If we can get Mr. Connor into the back seat, I can drive him into town."

"All right," Vivian said. "Go get your car. You'll need to open the gate."

It wasn't until after seven that Ted returned with Will, who had his leg in a cast and hobbled into the house on crutches. All the children except for Sally were in bed. Vivian had told her about Daddy's friend Ted and that he was wearing a uniform so she wouldn't mistake him for Earl as Will had.

Sally warmed up to Ted right away, taking his hand and leading him to the table where she'd set it for two. Vivian had a dinner of fried chicken and potatoes warming in the oven.

Will sat at the head of the table with his leg sticking out. "Doc said I'll be in the cast for three months." He put his head in his hands. "I'm so sorry, Vivian."

She stepped around the table and put her arms around him. "You have nothing to be sorry about. I'll see if I can hire someone."

"You know you can't afford to."

"Then we'll have to trust the Lord, won't we?"

Will nodded, ate his dinner, and then said he'd head to bed.

"I'll help you." Ted cleared his throat. "Sir, would you allow me to stay on your couch tonight? That way I can help you in the morning and do the chores too."

Will smiled a little. "Ask Vivian. She's the boss around here."

Ted turned toward her. "Vivian?"

"We'd appreciate that very much. Thank you. I'll get bedding for you."

After Ted finished helping Will to bed, he stopped in the living room.

"Whose car are you borrowing?" Vivian asked.

"I have a great-uncle who lives in Uhrichsville. I'm on my way home to Chicago from New York and decided stopping for a day would be my best opportunity to fulfill my promise to Earl. I hitched a ride from the train depot to borrow Uncle Joe's car and came up here. I'll return the car in the morning."

"Do you think he's worried about you?"

Ted grinned. "No, I think he's probably asleep without a care in the world." He stepped into the entryway and then returned with his rucksack. Again he pulled out the ball of yarn, scarf, and the letters. "Like I said, Earl asked that I deliver these in person if anything happened to him."

Vivian took the items from Ted.

Sally asked, "Did you knit that, Mama?"

"No." She gave Ted a puzzled look. "What is this?"

"Well, it seems to be a scarf, but beyond that I'm not sure. Earl got it while we were in Algiers, and he thought you would appreciate it."

"Why is the scarf still attached to the ball of yarn?"

Ted shrugged. "I have no idea." He picked up his rucksack and the pile of bedding Vivian had stacked for him on the sofa. "Thank you," he said.

Vivian paused and then said, "No, thank you." She held up the items in her hands. "For these and for helping Will. For doing the chores in the morning." She'd put the knitting project and letters in her bottom drawer, along with the letters from Ted. She'd deal with them later when she had more time.

"What will you do tomorrow after I leave?" Ted asked.

"I'll talk to the neighbors and see if they know of someone looking for work. We'll be all right."

Ted smiled. "You really are as strong as Earl said you were."

Tears threatened Vivian's eyes. She blinked them back and said, "Good night."

None of the neighbors knew of anyone looking for work, so Ted returned the car to his uncle and hitch-hiked back up to the farm, saying he'd stay until Vivian found a farmhand. With Will in the house and Sally able to help with the younger ones, Vivian and Ted finished up the fence the next day and then cleaned out the pigpen. They worked without talking except for Vivian giving Ted directions. For a city boy, he caught on quickly.

As they walked back out to the pigpen after lunch, Vivian noticed that Ted had a slight limp.

"Were you injured in the war?"

"The day after we lost Earl in the Battle of El Guettar, I took a bullet in my thigh," he said. "It got infected, which ended up being my ticket to England."

"Oh." Ted had been injured in the same battle Earl had died in. Vivian asked, "What happened after that?"

"I recovered and rejoined the 2nd Armored Division in England. We crossed the Channel and landed on Omaha Beach a few days after D-Day."

"Normandy."

He nodded.

"Were you on the Cotentin Peninsula? Anywhere near Saint-Vaast-la-Hougue?"

"Yes." Ted stopped walking. "How do you know about Normandy?"

"My sister's French family has—or had—a chateau there." She told him about Daisy and her wedding, how her husband was killed in the Battle of Singapore, and how Vivian hadn't heard from her sister since April 1942, over four years before.

Ted exhaled and said, "I'm sorry. There was so much loss. So much destruction."

"And you saw much of it, correct?"

He didn't answer.

Vivian said, "I followed the 2nd Armored Division in the news. I know from Tunisia, companies landed *on Sicily and then fought through Italy. Then other companies ended up in Normandy and fought through Germany and liberated concentration camps."*

"It was the vilest of wars," Ted said, his voice low and deep.

They started walking again, and after a minute Ted asked Vivian how she liked farm life.

"I love it," she said.

"Even though you're from London?"

She slowed her pace. "I do like the farm better than London," Vivian said. "Although I liked London too."

"Do you have any desire to go back?"

"Oh, no," Vivian said. "This is my home. This is where I'll stay, God willing, and raise my children. As long as I can keep this land."

That evening, after Ted helped Will get into bed, he went into the kitchen for a drink of water. The day had been hot, and the evening had barely cooled, but Vivian had the back door and windows open, hoping for a breeze. She took Ted's empty glass from him and said, "Thank you again for your help."

When he didn't answer, she turned toward him. His head was in his hands.

"What's wrong?" she asked.

He looked up and smiled a little. "Nothing. Good night." He stepped out the back door and then whistled as he descended the little knoll before the barn. There was a small room out there where previous farmhands had stayed before Earl and Vivian bought the place. Vivian had offered to let him stay in the house, but Ted said he felt more comfortable sleeping a bit rough. He still hadn't acclimated to being home on US soil.

Vivian wondered if Ted missed Earl. She did too, and even more so with Ted around.

One evening after supper, Sally put on a couple of her father's albums. The sound of the music made Vivian want to weep, and she was tempted to turn the phonograph off, but the children were already dancing. Vivian scooped Lottie up and swung her around. She did the same with EJ. Carol and Sally danced with each other. Ted stood on the edge of the room. Will grinned from ear to ear, ensconced in the easy chair with his casted leg outstretched. Soon, all of them were laughing. Then, as Vivian put EJ down, Ted stepped into the living room and said, "May I have this dance?"

Will continued grinning, and the children kept laughing. "Yes," she said, and extended her hand.

When Will's cast came off, he hobbled around on crutches for a week and then started walking with a cane. They sold the three-month-old piglets and got ready for two other sows to farrow. Then Ted and Vivian harvested the cabbage. The corn would be ready *in another month. One morning as Vivian walked out to the barn with Will, her father-in-law said, "The farm looks good. Ted is a good man."*

"Yes," Vivian answered.

"Earl would want you to be happy. Who better to make you happy than someone he trusted?"

Vivian's heart lurched.

"I'll never stop grieving Earl," Will said. "Nor will you, not completely. But I want you to be happy. Mary told me before she died that she hoped you would remarry, that the children would have another father. That you would have more children if God was willing. The best way for you to honor Earl is to live."

Vivian went into town the next day to see her mother. "What do you want to talk about?" Mum asked.

Vivian brushed tears from her eyes. "Earl. Daisy. How you ever figured out how to keep living, even with Daisy to care for, after your first husband died."

"You have to allow yourself to," Mum said. "You have to give yourself permission. Can you do that?"

"I think so," Vivian said.

"It's time," Mum said. "It's going on four years."

"I know."

Mum sighed. "And it's time we let Daisy go too. We would have heard from her if she was still alive."

"I know." Vivian couldn't stop the tears. Mum, unaffectionate as she was, wrapped her arms around Vivian. "I'm sorry," Vivian said. "I'm sorry for both of us."

"I know. So am I." Mum let go of Vivian. "I don't regret leaving London. But I do regret losing Daisy."

"We have each other," Vivian said.

"And your children," Mum replied.

After they harvested the corn, Ted chopped enough firewood to last the winter. As he and Vivian sat at the table one night, he said he needed to go to Chicago and see his mother and tend to some business. "Is there a chance you would want me to come back?"

"As a farmhand or something more?"

"Something more," he answered.

"Something more to save the farm, or to be a husband because you love me?"

He reached for her hand. "Definitely the latter." He held it only a moment before he let it go. "But don't answer now." He took a piece of paper from his pocket. "I've written down my mother's address in Chicago where I'll be staying. Think about what you want—truly want. And then write me a letter."

"What do you want?"

"You." He spread his arms wide. "And this. All of this. But only if you want me."

After Ted went out to the barn and the children were all in bed, Vivian took her and Earl's letters from her bottom drawer, along with the odd knitting project with the scarf and ball of yarn still attached. She hadn't looked at it since the day Ted arrived. She put all the letters in chronological order and then read through them, noting Earl's mention of having gotten a gift for her but not being able to write about it. After that, he wrote about Ted, who was both capable and dependable. Already, I trust him with my life. Ted was like the brother Earl had never had. He and I are the oldest in our squad. We have each other's backs.

Earl had seen Ted under intense pressure and found him worthy. He had talked at length to Ted about her and the children. He saw him as a brother. Earl was a good judge of character—and so was she. Ted had been tried by war. He'd had his best friend killed beside him. Surely he had dark moments, and yet he was stable enough to care for his friend's wife, children, father, and farm for five months, insisting he sleep in the barn the entire time instead of going home to Chicago or to his uncle in Uhrichsville.

Yes, Ted Johnston was a good man. Did she feel the way she did at seventeen when she first met Earl

Connor? No. But she'd come to love Ted over the last five months, working side by side. Caring for Will. Caring for the children.

And he showed her that he cared for all of them, every day.

She turned her attention to the knitting project. Why would Earl keep it for her? The yarn was primitive and barely spun. The needles were old. She ran her hands over the bumpy scarf. The mix of knit and purl stitches didn't make a pattern. She thought of Daisy telling her about the woman in Belgium, who'd knitted the train schedules and passed on the information. She thought of the scarf she'd made for Earl, that had most likely been buried with him.

Daisy knew Morse code. She'd tried to teach it to Vivian. What did she remember? Will had put his few books in Vivian's bookcase. Did he have a book on Morse code from when he worked for the railroad? She went out to the living room and searched, book by book. There was a pamphlet between an accounting book and a world history book, both of which Will had used in high school. Vivian pulled out the pamphlet. On the cover was printed Morse Code. *She grabbed a piece of paper and a pencil from the desk and hurried back to her bedroom to decode the message.*

inside

ball

use

for

children

remember

who

taught

you

to

knit

She pulled the knitting needles out of the ball of yarn and unwound it.

Daisy's ring! Earl had seen Daisy! Mum had told him to look for her, but what were the chances he would have found her? Had Daisy gone back to France after North Africa was taken by the Allies? Had Ted been near her in Normandy after Earl died? Ted wouldn't have known to look for her—and Vivian doubted she would ever know what happened to her sister.

Vivian lay down on her bed, still holding the ring. Why would Daisy have sent it? Perhaps it was too painful for her to keep. Should she tell Mum about it? Then Daddy would know, and they would both insist she get it appraised and probably sell it. Daisy wanted her to use the money for her children.

What should she do?

If one of the children fell ill or she was about to lose the farm, she would get an appraisal and sell the ring. In the meantime, she'd leave it in her bottom dresser drawer in the ball of yarn. Sally was the only one who knew about the scarf. There was no need to tell the other children. No one needed to know about the ring.

Vivian held up her left hand, looking at the gold band she wore from Earl. She took it off and put it in her jewelry box. She'd save it for EJ to give his wife someday. She breathed a prayer for her future. She loved Ted. She was ready to join her life with his. If that was what the Lord wanted for her.

The next morning a sleepy-eyed EJ asked, "Where is Ted? I want Ted."

Will, who sat at his place at the table, gave Vivian a smile.

"Ted went to Chicago," Vivian said.

"But he's coming back," Lottie said matter-of-factly. When Vivian didn't answer, Lottie asked, "Right, Mama?"

"Yes," Vivian said. "He's coming back."

That night she wrote him a letter, saying that she'd made her decision.

I love you, Ted. I want to share my life with you. I want you to be my husband. I want you to be a father to my children. I want to farm this land with you. Perhaps we'll always feel a little guilty we'll have the life Earl wanted, but that's all the more reason for us both to make the most of the life we have now. It's what I want—but it's what Earl would have wanted too.

Four days later she had her response from Ted in a short note.

I can't express how happy I was to receive your letter. I'm putting all of my business in order here. My mother recently sold a valuable ring, which means she shouldn't have financial difficulties in the years to come. I've informed her of our decision, and I've purchased a gold wedding band for you. God willing, you'll be in my arms by Friday.

It was Friday! He didn't ask her to pick him up at the station, and she had no idea which train he'd be on. She hurried to the house as the wintry wind whipped the skirt of her work dress. She'd finished the afternoon chores, and a pot of stew simmered on the stove. Sally was home from school and playing with the younger children, and Will sat in the rocking chair reading the newspaper. Vivian quickly changed her dress. It was too cold for Ted to sleep in the barn anymore—she'd make up a room upstairs for him. When all of that was done, she came down the stairs and heard "Now You're in My Arms" playing on the phonograph. Sally must have put it on. Vivian stepped from the hall to the living room just as a knock fell on the front door.

"I'll get it!" Carol shouted, sliding on the hardwood floor in her stocking feet. Then she called out, "Ted!"

All the children rushed to him. He scooped EJ up into his arms and hugged each of the girls one by one as the music played.

"Where's your mama?" he finally asked, putting EJ down and pulling away from the girls.

Vivian stepped forward. Ted moved closer with Lottie and EJ hanging onto his legs. As Ted took Vivian's hand, he asked, "Will you marry me?"

"Yes." She couldn't stop the tears. "Absolutely, yes."

The song came to an end as Ted took Vivian in his arms.

CHAPTER TWENTY-ONE

*D*ebbie woke up the next morning thinking about Vivian and Ted. The four children. The three more babies Vivian had with Ted. Talk about beauty from ashes.

Her heart swelled as she climbed out of bed. She wanted her life with Greg to be a beauty from ashes story too. She'd lost her fiancé, and Greg had lost his wife. They had both grieved and struggled and grown through the years since. Then they'd met, started dating, and brought a new kind of joy to each other.

Or did, until he started acting distant, off and on. She needed to talk with him about what she'd deciphered from Vivian's boxes the night before. Maybe she'd just come right out and ask him what was troubling him. She'd try to catch a couple of minutes with him before the dance.

The morning sped by—until just before eleven when Debbie turned to see a man coming toward her with two vases full of plush pink roses.

"Deliveries, one for Janet and one for Debbie," he said.

Debbie took the vases and set them on a nearby table. Janet came out of the kitchen, grinning broadly. She had a few bills in her hand and tipped the delivery guy.

"Our guys either coordinated with the florist, or this is one coincidence we'll be talking about for years," Janet said dryly.

Debbie just grinned, then buried her nose in one fragrant bloom. "These are gorgeous, aren't they?" She'd chosen the right bouquet, because when she opened the card, it was addressed to her. *Happy Valentine's Day, Valentine. Let's dance the night away.* She felt her heart swell. Whatever was occupying his thoughts these days, at least he was still thinking about her too.

Later, just before Debbie closed the café, after Janet and Paulette had left, Kim came into the café for a cup of coffee. "I have an update for you." She put the note on the counter. "My friend has access to a database of typefaces, new and old. The size and shape of the letters vary from model to model, making it possible to identify the make and model of the typewriter." She sat down at the counter. "According to her, the note was typed on a 1950 Underwood typewriter and, by following up on the watermark, she determined that the paper was manufactured in the late 1980s. Also, the ink appears to have faded, so unless someone forged the note and knew exactly what to do, it's the real deal."

"Thank you." Debbie poured coffee into a paper to-go cup and put a lid on it.

"Of course, if any of your suspects has a 1950 Underwood typewriter and knows how to make ink look faded…" Her voice trailed off.

Debbie laughed and put the coffee on the counter. "Not that I know of."

"Then," Kim said, "you have your answer."

"Thank you," Debbie said. "And thank you for asking me to work on the home front exhibit. I can't tell you how much I've enjoyed reading Vivian's diaries and letters and piecing through her life. I ended up having the privilege of getting to know Greg's grandmother and grandfathers and also his father and three of his siblings as little ones. Along with all four of his great-grandparents. Anyway, I have more photos for you. Plus, I'll type up quotes from her about her knitting circle and what it was like to be a young widow and her life on the farm. I'll email a document to you by Tuesday morning."

"Great." Kim picked up the cup. "I'll have the exhibit up by the end of the month."

"Nice." Debbie wiped her hands on her apron. "I'll let Paulette and Greg know. And Sally and Lottie too."

Kim stood. "We're looking forward to the dance tonight."

Debbie gave Kim a wave. "See you soon."

As Debbie left the café, she decided to go by Greg's neighborhood and ask if anyone had seen Meg's pickup the day the boxes appeared on Greg's porch. If she could put Meg in the vicinity of Greg's house that day, it would make her feel more comfortable identifying Meg as the most likely person to have planted the yarn and ring in the box on Greg's porch.

She checked the houses on both sides of Greg's, but no one was home. Then she went one door down, and a man that she'd seen occasionally in the café answered. He grinned. "Debbie, how can I help you?"

"This is an odd question, but were you home on Saturday, February first, during the afternoon?"

"Why yes," he said. "I probably was. There was a lot of shoveling to do two Saturdays ago."

"Did you happen to see a red king cab pickup in the neighborhood?"

He squinted and then said, "Can't say that I did. I probably would have noticed it. Not many people were out, and our street is pretty narrow."

"All right." Debbie smiled. "Thank you."

He chuckled. "I hope you find what you're looking for."

So did she. She knocked on the next door, but again no one was home.

There was an older woman outside across the street. Debbie headed toward her. "Hello," she said. Debbie asked her the same question.

"Actually," the woman said. "I did see a red pickup. A woman parked it in the driveway of the Connor house and ran up to their back porch. She was only there a moment and then drove away. Meg Sinclair is who it was."

Debbie nearly choked. "Are you sure?"

"Positive. I moved into town about a year ago after my husband died. Meg used to drive by our farm all the time, and sometimes she'd check to see if we needed anything. Really nice woman. I had no idea she knew the Connors." The woman motioned to Greg's house. "Don't say anything, but I sure enjoy watching Greg and the boys and their comings and goings. I'm old and it's just so nice to see young people, including Greg."

"I won't say anything." Debbie extended her hand. "I'm Debbie, a friend of Greg's."

The woman grinned. "I know. I see you all the time too. I'm Midge." Then she glanced past Debbie. "Look who's home."

Greg turned into his driveway but didn't open the garage door.

Debbie gave Midge a wave and said, "Nice to meet you!" Then she jogged across the street.

Greg climbed down from his truck but didn't see her.

She called out, "Hey!"

He turned with a surprised look on his face. "Debbie."

"Do you have a minute?"

"I was just going to grab something inside and go get Julian. So I have about ten minutes."

"I'll wait out here," Debbie said. "In the truck."

He returned in a ridiculously short amount of time. As he climbed into the truck, he asked, "What's up?"

"First, the flowers are gorgeous. Thank you."

He smiled. "I figured I couldn't go wrong with pink."

"Did you help Ian decide on pink too?"

He hesitated, as if cooking up some story, but then he laughed. "Busted. We thought it would be fun for you two to get matching bouquets. I hope that was okay."

"More than okay," Debbie said, grinning. "We got a big kick out of it. Pretty sure the customers did too." She held up her left hand and started counting down on her fingers. "I have updates. One, who planted the knitting in the box on your porch; two, where the yarn and ring originated; three, how they came into your grandmother's possession; four, who your grandmother wanted to have the ring; and five"—she pulled on her thumb—"the sweetest love story I've ever heard."

"Wow," Greg said.

"I'll give you the quick version. One, Meg Sinclair."

"You're kidding?"

"No." Debbie continued. "Two, Daisy Dumont Chapman, your great-aunt, and your grandfather saw each other in Algeria, and she gave him the knitting project with the ring in the ball of yarn. Three, Ted brought them with him at your grandfather's request when he stopped by the farm in June of 1946. Four, a colleague of Kim's verified that the note I found signed by your grandmother is genuine, as long as all can verify the signature. Five, your grandmother had two epic great loves, your grandfather and Ted, but it was all one story. And one song—'Now You're in My Arms.'"

"Wow," Greg said again. "My head is spinning."

Debbie explained that Midge had seen Meg park and then run up to Greg's back porch the day Paulette dropped the boxes off.

Greg gripped the steering wheel. "I don't want to confront her at the dance."

"I don't either," Debbie said. "I still haven't figured out how she knew the boxes would be on your porch. It would probably be good to have that piece of the puzzle in place before anyone speaks with her." Debbie put her hand over Greg's. "Let's see what happens once she sees the photo. Maybe she'll come clean." Then Debbie pulled out the note from Vivian about the ring. "You should keep this."

"That looks like Grandma's handwriting, from what I can remember. I'll stop by and show Mom and see what she says. I'll tell her about Meg too."

"Good idea." Debbie leaned closer to him. "And now for some good news."

"Better than you figuring all of this out?"

Debbie laughed. "Maybe not better, but your aunt Lottie is in town."

He grinned. "Is she?"

"She's going to be at the dance with Katherine and Sally."

"Nice," he said. "Lottie is a lot of fun. Mom plans to come too."
Debbie knew that. "And Jaxon and Julian."

Debbie hadn't known that. She reached for the door handle. "Okay, I'll go so you can get Julian. See you at seven."

"See you then."

When she arrived home, Debbie made a cup of tea and then sank into her comfy chair. She needed a minute. But she couldn't stop thinking about Ted. He'd been on the Cotentin Peninsula in Normandy with the knitting project and ring in his rucksack at the same time that Daisy may have been. But he didn't know to look for the Dumont chateau, as Charlotte had instructed Earl to do.

And most likely, Daisy was already dead by then.

She thought of Vivian's prayer about Ted. Debbie felt the same way about Greg. Just like Vivian, she needed to trust the Lord. Whatever His plans for her, she'd follow Him.

Debbie arrived at the depot at six, wearing her red dress with the flared skirt. She'd painted her fingernails red and wore her brightest red lipstick too. Janet was already putting out the cookies and other goodies on the table. They would both take turns, along with Paulette, serving soft drinks, coffee, and hot chocolate in the café.

"Ooh, la la." Janet grinned. "Look at you." Janet wore a black dress with her heart apron over the top and red hoop earrings. A red clip pulled her blond hair back on the right side of her head. "Go get your apron," Janet said. "We don't want to mess up our dresses."

Debbie put her purse in the cupboard in the café, hung up her coat, and put on her apron. When she stepped back into the lobby, Janet asked, "Has it started to snow yet?"

"Not yet." Debbie tied her apron as she spoke. "But it's cold enough to." She glanced over at the scrapbook display. "Greg doesn't want to confront Meg tonight."

Janet placed the last cookie on the tray on a serving plate. "Should I put the display away?"

"No." Debbie picked up the tray. "Let's see what happens. I'll go grab the tray of chocolate cheesecake hearts."

The DJ showed up a few minutes later, followed by Kim. "Where's Barry?" Debbie asked.

"He's resting but hopes to come a little later." Kim headed toward the museum. "I'll be back in a few minutes."

Paulette arrived next and headed into the café to get everything ready to serve beverages.

A bus of residents from Good Shepherd arrived at ten of seven, including Ray and Eileen. A couple minutes later, Sally, Katherine, and Lottie swooped in, all dressed to the nines.

Debbie decided there was no time like the present to show Katherine the photo of Ted's letter to Vivian. She approached her, saying, "I found a clue about the Johnston ring. I took a photo." She pulled up the photo and handed her phone to Katherine. "Ted went to Chicago in the spring of 1947 before he and Vivian married. He wrote to her saying he'd purchased a gold band. He also said that his mother had sold a valuable ring, which meant she wouldn't have financial problems for some time. Does it seem plausible she would have sold the ring and told Ted but not your father?"

Katherine glanced up from the phone with an expression of remorse on her face. "Yes. Dad was always far more materialistic than Ted. I should have remembered that when I was so sure Ted took the ring for Vivian." She turned to Lottie and then to Sally. "I'm sorry."

Sally said, "Don't give it another thought."

As Debbie took her phone back, Meg and Jeff waltzed into the lobby. Meg brushed the shoulders of her coat. "It's starting to snow!"

Meg spoke with the DJ, the lights dimmed, and the DJ started the music. The first song was Bennie Goodman's "Let's Dance." Meg and Jeff took to the floor.

"When will Ian be here?" Debbie asked Janet.

"Soon." She shrugged. "Which means, who knows? I'm used to police business sometimes taking precedence. It's fine."

"Go take a turn in the café and tell Paulette to come on out. That way you'll have done your turn by the time he arrives."

"What about you?" Janet asked.

"Greg isn't here yet."

"He will be."

"I'll take a turn after you."

A few minutes later, Paulette joined Debbie by the table of goodies. "Are Greg and the boys here yet?"

"Not yet," Debbie said.

"They're probably having a tie-tying lesson."

Debbie smiled. "That, I would like to see."

Paulette laughed. "So would I." She leaned toward Debbie. "Greg stopped by with an update about Vivian's ring, etc., and the knitting project. I can't thank you enough. You did everyone a big favor."

"Well, it's not over yet. Someone still needs to talk with Meg. We should hear her side of the story."

"We will," Paulette said. "When the time is right."

A few minutes later, Greg came in with Jaxon and Julian trailing behind him. Lottie yelled out, "Greg!" from the table where she and Sally and Katherine sat. She hopped up and hurried over to him, giving him a big hug. He introduced her to Julian and Jaxon, and Lottie gave each of them a hug too.

Greg nodded at Paulette, and Jaxon came over to her. He said hello to Debbie and then said, "Grandma, I watched some videos online about swing dancing. Do you want to give it a try?"

"Absolutely," Paulette said.

Debbie watched them walk onto the dance floor and stop near Lottie, who had pulled Julian out on the floor.

Greg walked up to Debbie with a grin on his face. "May I have this dance?" he asked.

"Of course." She extended her hand.

Greg took it and led her onto the dance floor.

The evening sped by as fast as the Lindy Hop. Debbie danced with Greg and with Ian when he arrived. She took a turn serving drinks in the café and then watched Kim and Barry, who had finally arrived, dance to a slower song. She watched Eileen push Ray's chair from side to side and Greg dance with each of his aunts and Katherine. The floor grew more crowded as the night continued, with all ages, from five to a hundred years old, enjoying the dancing.

Patricia and Harry arrived, along with Crosby, and Patricia's parents, Vernon and Ruth. Harry visited with people, but Patricia danced with Ian and Greg and her dad.

To Debbie's complete surprise, her parents walked into the lobby at eight thirty, both dressed in formal attire, Dad in his tuxedo and Mom in a long peach dress with a slit at the ankle. She hurried over to hug them both. "Sorry we're late," Mom said.

"I didn't even know you were coming," Debbie gushed. "You both look fabulous."

At nine, Meg took the microphone and announced the dance contest. "Eileen Palmer, Harry Franklin, and Ray Zink, who have the most experience with swing dancing of any of us, will be the judges."

The DJ directed the spotlight to the three seniors, who all sat at the same table. Each waved.

"All are welcome to join in the contest. The winning couple will receive a free dinner for two at Buona Vita!"

Greg grabbed Debbie's hand and said, "Are you game?"

She laughed. "I guess so, if you're sure you don't mind me stepping on your toes again."

"Never."

Everyone danced their hearts out, song after song. Couples were eliminated, including Debbie and Greg after a few too many stepping-on-toes incidents, until only Meg and Jeff and Janet and Ian were left.

The last song was Glenn Miller's "Chattanooga Choo Choo," one of the most beloved World War II songs of all. Debbie wished she'd requested "Now You're in My Arms" at some point. Now the evening was almost over.

Janet and Ian did their best, but even though they were twenty years younger, they were no match for Meg and Jeff. Eileen spoke with the DJ, who landed the spotlight on Meg and Jeff and announced them as the winners.

Everyone clapped, and the DJ invited everyone else onto the dance floor one more time. Bennie Goodman's "Moonglow" came over the loudspeakers.

Debbie pulled Greg away from the floor. "What would you like to drink?" she asked. "I'll get it."

When she came out of the café with two waters, Jeff and Meg stood at the scrapbook display, looking at the photos from the last year.

Meg turned, looked at Debbie and then at Sally and Lottie and Katherine and Paulette, who had gathered behind her. Meg put her head in her hands for a long moment, looked up, and said, "I'm so sorry. I had no idea there was a ring in that ball of yarn, and when I found it I thought it was costume jewelry. The stone wasn't even bright. I never would have worn it to the dance last year if I thought it was worth anything."

"It's a cushion cut," Katherine said. "Which makes it a little dull."

"I only took the scarf and yarn because I didn't think anyone wanted it." Meg wrapped her arms around herself. "I was so mortified when Katherine came around asking questions about a valuable ring—"

"Wait." Debbie turned toward Katherine. "You went to Meg's and asked her about the ring?"

"I did," Katherine said. "And I told her Paulette was getting together Vivian's diaries, letters, and loose photographs to give to Greg. That she had everything in a storage unit."

Debbie asked Meg, "But how did you know the boxes would be on Greg's porch?"

"I went to the storage units that morning, hoping to figure out how to get the items into Paulette's unit, when I saw her put boxes in her car. So I followed her to Greg's. I was afraid to go up to the house in the morning, but by afternoon, I figured I'd look to see if the boxes were still on the porch. I wouldn't have another chance to put the yarn with Vivian's things and undo what I'd done." Meg wrapped her arms around herself. "But I only made things worse." She looked around the semicircle of people from the Connor-Johnston family. "What do I need to do to make this right?"

Sally stepped forward. "Nothing. Thank you for being honest. I believe you."

"What will happen to the ring?" Meg asked.

Greg took a jewelry box out of his pocket. "Debbie found a note from Grandma saying she wanted Sally to have the ring." He handed his aunt the box. Then he pulled an envelope from his inside pocket. "Here's the note from Grandma and the information from the appraisal."

Sally began to cry and hugged Greg. After a long minute, Lottie put her arm around her sister and said, "Let's go touch up your makeup."

Debbie focused on cleaning up as people began to leave. Once the treat tables were clear, she realized the DJ hadn't packed up. And there were still quite a few people in the depot.

The DJ spoke into his microphone. "It turns out, I have one more song to play."

Greg was at Debbie's side, taking her hand as "Now You're in My Arms" began to play. He took her in his arms as Gene Austin began to croon. As they stepped forward and backward, Debbie noticed her parents on the side of the dance floor watching. Hadn't they seen enough of her and Greg dancing already during the contest?

Jaxon and Julian stood on the other side. Janet and Ian stepped next to them.

Debbie concentrated on her dancing, following Greg's lead without stumbling once. As the last line played, Greg whispered, "…and now you're in my arms." He pulled her close and then extended his hand and hers, holding them high. Debbie twirled under them.

Then, still holding her hand, Greg cleared his throat. "I have something important I want to say to you."

Debbie's heart skipped a beat. Was it her imagination or was everyone stepping closer, forming a circle around them?

Greg spoke clearly. "From the first day we met I knew you were special, but I couldn't have predicted I would fall head over heels in love with you. It didn't take long to know you were the one for me. Your love for your family and friends, your dedication to serving others, and your love of the past, present, and future have all inspired me. I hope you'll have me as your husband. I hope today will be the beginning of a deepening love and precious commitment that will sustain us in the years to come."

Greg took a ring box out of his jacket pocket and dropped to one knee.

Debbie's hand flew to her mouth. He was really proposing! In front of all their friends and family.

Greg opened the box, revealing the snowflake ring from the appraiser's office. How had he known?

Her hand dropped from her mouth as she gasped.

Greg's blue eyes met hers. "Debbie." He paused a moment, holding her gaze with his. "Will you marry me?"

"Yes." She choked back her tears. "I love you, Greg. Of course I'll marry you."

He took the ring from the box and slipped it on her finger. Everyone began to clap and cheer as Debbie took Greg's hand in hers and helped him up.

Then she tilted her head up toward his, and they kissed. And then hugged. And kissed again.

When they broke apart, she saw that Jaxon and Julian stood behind him. Mom and Dad had stepped to Debbie's left.

The song started again. Mom hugged Debbie, and Dad shook Greg's hand. Janet stood a few steps away, beaming. She blew Debbie a kiss, which Debbie returned. Then Debbie turned to Jaxon and Julian. Jaxon gave her a thumbs-up and stepped forward to hug her. Debbie hugged him back and then pulled a grinning Julian into a hug too. Greg wrapped his arms around all three of them, holding them tight and then pulling way, taking Debbie's right hand.

He twirled Debbie and then took her into his arms as the last line played again.

Dear Reader,

Happy February! And more specifically, Happy Valentine's Day!

I loved writing *Now You're in My Arms*—and especially Greg's contemporary wedding proposal to Debbie. What could be more romantic for a couple than a retro 1940s swing dance in the lobby of a historic depot with all their loved ones gathered around?

But what was both fun and challenging for me in writing this story was going back in history to Greg's grandmother Vivian and her life in the 1940s.

First, a little bit about my inspiration for Vivian, which is every woman I know who has ever sent her husband off to war—including myself. I've been married forty years to my sweetheart, who proposed in a rose garden when we were only twenty and twenty-two. I survived said sweetheart's thirty years in the Army Reserve, including one year in a combat zone. We raised four wonderful people into adulthood during those thirty years and now cherish and nurture our beloved grandbabies.

Because of my age and experience, I definitely found Vivian to be the heart of this story.

Like me, my fictional character married young, had four children, and sent her husband off to war. But unlike mine, Vivian's husband doesn't return. But this young woman, in the midst of her life-altering grief, trusts in the Lord and keeps moving forward. She falls in love again and has three more children. She forges a strong second marriage and raises her family. Although she never forgets her first love, she keeps moving forward.

And under the influence of Vivian's faithfulness, strength, and perseverance, her grandson Greg—long after his grandmother has passed—is equipped to deal with the death of a spouse, raise his sons in the faith, and to embrace a second chance at love—with Debbie.

We have no idea as we're living what our legacy will be, but if we live out our faith in love as Vivian did, no doubt God will bring good things to those descendants who follow after us.

I hope Greg's proposal to Debbie brought this story full circle for you, as it did for me.

Enjoy!

Leslie Gould

ABOUT the AUTHOR

*L*eslie Gould is the number-one bestselling and Christy-Award winning author of over forty novels. She's also won two Faith, Hope, and Love Readers' Choice Awards and a *Romantic Times* Reviewers' Choice Inspirational Novel of the Year Award. Leslie has a bachelor's degree in history and a Master of Fine Arts degree in creative writing. In the past, she's taught writing at the university level, curated the Swedenburg House Museum in Ashland, Oregon, and edited a magazine in Portland, Oregon. Currently, she writes and edits full-time. She and her husband, Peter, live in Oregon and enjoy hiking, traveling, and spending time with their four adult children and two grandchildren.

TRUTH BEHIND the FICTION

Who isn't fascinated by spies? I know I am! As I outlined *Now You're in My Arms*, the intrigue of including female spies in the story captivated my imagination and sent me on a research frenzy. I found a plethora of fascinating information. Two books that were especially helpful were *Agent Josephine: American Beauty, French Hero, British Spy* by Damien Lewis and *D-Day Girls: The Spies Who Armed the Resistance, Sabotaged the Nazis, and Helped Win World War II* by Sarah Rose.

The British reluctantly recruited women as spies and saboteurs. There was a shortage of men to serve as spies because most had been conscripted into the military, plus stereotypes made women less conspicuous than men. Who would suspect a woman of planting a bomb to blow up a train tunnel? Or sending intelligence by knitting code into a sweater?

Female spies operated in North Africa during the German and Italian occupation, in collaboration with the French Vichy Government. The most famous female spy was Josephine Baker, an American-born French singer and dancer. Alarmed by the discrimination she witnessed under fascism, she vowed to help free France any way she could, first by spying on Axis countries at Japanese and Italian embassy parties and then, in 1941, by relocating to Morocco to set up a transmission center in Casablanca. She wrote messages on her arms, hid notes in her bra, and wrote intelligence on music sheets in invisible ink during her spy career. There were other women also spying in North Africa for the Allies at the time, including an artist in Algeria.

After the liberation of France, Josephine returned to Paris in October 1944 as a heroine. She received two of France's highest military honors for her service. Her story and stories of other female spies inspired me to place Daisy in Algeria in 1942 and '43.

Starting in 1942, women who were fluent in both the French language and the French culture and had gone through extensive training through the British Special Operations Executive began parachuting into France during full moons and continued to serve in the country until the Allies liberated France in 1944. The spies worked with the French Resistance to help prepare the way for the D-Day invasion through collecting intelligence on German troop movements and activities and sabotaging German infrastructure. Some World War II experts estimate the spies reduced the length of the war by as much as a year, saving countless lives. But it came at a heavy cost. The Nazis captured and sent many of the spies to concentration camps, where few survived until the end of the war, while others were executed. Virginia Hall, an America socialite from Baltimore, was an Allied spy in France who survived and later worked for the CIA.

Overall, the fatality rate for female spies in France was forty-two percent.

I hope *Now You're in My Arms* not only honors the millions of Allied soldiers who died during World War II but also the brave women who sacrificed their lives too.

FROM *the* HOME-FRONT KITCHEN

Janet's Chocolate Peanut Butter Cheesecake Bars

Ingredients:

Crust

20 crème-filled chocolate sandwich cookies (like Oreos)

½ tablespoon butter, melted

Filling

16 ounce brick cream cheese, room temperature

1 cup granulated sugar

1 cup creamy peanut butter

3 large eggs, room temperature

1 teaspoon vanilla extract

¼ teaspoon salt

3 tablespoons all-purpose flour

hot water

Chocolate Topping

½ cup unsalted butter

1 heaping cup semisweet chocolate chips

Directions:

Preheat oven to 350 degrees. Line an 8×8-inch baking pan with baking parchment or aluminum foil, allowing overhang. Lightly coat with cooking spray.

Pulse cookies in food processor until fully ground. Continue pulsing while gradually streaming in melted butter until incorporated. Press mixture evenly into prepared baking pan. Bake 10 minutes. Set aside and allow to cool about 10 minutes.

Using an electric mixer on medium speed, beat together cream cheese and sugar until smooth. Mix in peanut butter, then eggs, one at a time; beat together until smooth. Add vanilla, salt, and flour, beating until just combined. Pour evenly over prepared crust. Place pan on large, rimmed baking sheet and place in oven on center rack. Pour hot water into baking sheet until almost full. Bake at 350 degrees for about 40 to 45 minutes, until set around edges but still slightly jiggly in middle.

Remove the pan and cool completely on rack. Once cool, cover and chill until firm, at least 3 hours.

For chocolate topping: Cut butter into tablespoon-size pieces. Place into a heat-proof bowl. Pour chocolate chips on top. Place in the microwave and melt in 30-second increments until smooth, stirring after each. Let the mixture cool for 2 to 3 minutes, then pour and spread evenly over chilled cheesecake bars. Using the parchment or foil overhang, lift cheesecake out of pan and cut to desired size.

*Read on for a sneak peek of another exciting book
in the* Whistle Stop Café Mysteries *series!*

SOONER OR LATER

BY BETH ADAMS

*J*anet Shaw was just about finished wiping down the counters when Debbie Albright's phone rang. It was a gray March Monday, the bitter wind whipping around outside, but it was cozy and warm inside the Whistle Stop Café. The lunch rush was over, and they were almost finished cleaning up. They had just sent Paulette Connor, who waited tables for them, home, and Janet was looking forward to getting home herself and spending the rest of the afternoon getting started on a project she'd been planning for quite a while. As the bleat of Debbie's cell phone sounded again, Debbie rested her broom against the wall of the dining room and pulled the phone out of her pocket.

"Hey there," Debbie said into the phone.

It was Greg. Janet could tell just by the way Debbie's voice softened and her lips curled up into a smile. Debbie and Greg Connor had been dating for several months, and just a few weeks ago Greg had proposed. Janet couldn't be happier for her best friend, and she loved seeing how Debbie lit up whenever Greg called.

"What?" Debbie said into the phone. "That's crazy."

Janet couldn't hear what Greg was saying, but whatever it was, Debbie was obviously surprised.

"Where?"

Janet finished wiping the counter and rinsed out her rag in the bucket of warm water, watching Debbie the whole time. Janet had already stacked the leftover pastries and wrapped them to take home, and Debbie had broken down the register and transferred the cash to the safe in the office. She'd also taken copies of many of the recipes they used in the kitchen at various points in the day while her partner was busy with other tasks, and she was ready to go home and start working on her project. As soon as Debbie finished in the dining room, they should be ready to head out.

"I can't believe it," Debbie was saying. "I think there is one, but I don't know if it's the right kind or if it works. I can ask Kim and let you know." After another pause she said, "Okay. I'll go talk to her now and let you know."

She ended the call and turned to Janet. "That was Greg."

"I'd gathered that. What's going on?"

"He's renovating the old theater over on Grant."

"I wondered what was happening there. Is someone actually going to turn it back into a theater again?" The old building must have been beautiful once, but the marquee outside the long, low brick building had long since been battered and broken, and the building abandoned. Janet remembered the space being used as a discount clothing store and a short-lived bank over the years. For a while a church had met there until they'd built their own building outside of town. But mostly it had sat empty, an eyesore.

"Jim Watson's brother Sam bought it," Debbie said. Jim was the editor of the *Gazette,* the local newspaper. "He plans to turn it back into a theater, and Greg is working on the renovations."

"That's wonderful. It will be so nice to have a local theater again." Greg was a contractor, and he would do a great job of restoring the old place. "But it sounds like something exciting happened in the process?"

"Greg said he was knocking down some walls today, and in the space inside one wall, he found some old film canisters. Like, movie film strips. One of the canisters has a date written on it—September 1944."

"Whoa. I knew that theater was old, but I didn't know it was that old."

"I think Greg said it opened back in the thirties originally. Obviously it underwent a lot of changes as technology progressed, but anyway, it's possible that at least one of the rolls of film could be from the forties. He thought he remembered seeing an old film projector at the museum, and wondered if it might still work."

"Huh. There is one there, right?" Janet could picture the hulking machine. It was in one of the back rooms of the museum, in a display about films centered on World War II. "Does it work?"

"I have no idea, but I said I would ask Kim. I haven't seen her yet today, so I don't know if she's around."

The museum was closed on Mondays. But this sounded like the kind of thing Kim Smith would be excited about. "Let's give her a call. If it is old film from the forties, she'll be interested to learn more."

Debbie nodded and pulled up the Dennison Depot Museum director's phone number and made the call. Janet listened in on Debbie's end of the conversation as she explained what Greg had found and what they were looking for. When Debbie hung up, she had a smile on her face.

"She was at home and said this is much more interesting than folding laundry. She'll be right over. I'll tell Greg to bring the film here."

Janet hesitated. What she was about to say seemed kind of crazy, but she decided to just say it. "You don't think there's any chance it's *that* film, do you?"

"The Clark Gable film?" Debbie asked. The fact that Debbie knew what she was talking about meant that she'd thought of it too.

"Didn't it disappear about that time?" Janet had heard about the film star's visit to Dennison many times over the years. Clark Gable, one of Hollywood's biggest celebrities, had been born in nearby Cadiz and enlisted in the army during World War II. After he'd been discharged from active military duty, he'd come back to Ohio and spent nearly two weeks in Dennison, filming footage for a movie he planned to make about the war effort on the home front. But after a week and a half of shooting, the film was stolen from his hotel room and never recovered. The project was abandoned, the star left town, and the missing film had never been found. Many of the older residents in town still referenced the star's visit to Dennison from time to time, and they'd all heard the story.

"I think 1944 was about the time the film was stolen, if I'm remembering correctly," Debbie said. "I don't know. I guess what Greg found could be that film, but it doesn't make any sense. How would it have ended up inside the wall of the theater in Dennison if it was the film stolen from Clark Gable?"

"I don't know," Janet said. "I guess we'll have to see what it is if we can get the projector working."

By the time Janet and Debbie had finished cleaning up the café, Kim had arrived to unlock the museum, and Janet and Debbie walked through the old station waiting room and into the museum entrance. Kim greeted them and flipped on the overhead lights and then led them through the quiet museum to one of the rooms at the back.

"Here it is," Kim said, gesturing at a large machine that was nearly the size of a person. The top part was a metal case with a series of lenses at the front. The bottom was a large metal box, where Janet assumed the motor was housed.

"I knew I'd seen it here," Debbie said.

"Does it work?" Janet asked.

"It's supposed to," Kim said. "It's a 1940s-era 35mm projector. I rescued it from the old theater decades ago, back when they were turning it into a bank. It had been sitting in the basement in storage for years, and Stanley said it should still work, but to be honest I've never tried it."

"Stanley?" Debbie blinked.

"Stanley Hersey," Kim said. "He owned the theater until it closed in the eighties."

Janet had heard that name before. She thought Stanley was the father of Max Hersey, her dad's childhood friend.

"He was clearing out the storage rooms before he sold the building," Kim continued. "I swooped in to rescue as much as I could.

This beauty was a real modern marvel in her day. Let's see if we can fire her up."

Kim unlocked the glass case that held the projector. Janet looked at the display around it and saw that it showcased stories of Hollywood stars who were also active-duty service members. There was a black-and-white photo of Jimmy Stewart in his Army uniform, and the paragraphs underneath the photo discussed the film star's illustrious military career. Stewart, Janet read, was already a big star when he'd enlisted in the army in 1941, and he'd fought in the European theater during the war. He'd retired from the military as a Brigadier General, making him the highest-ranking actor in American military history. There were also sections of the display dedicated to Audie Murphy, Bea Arthur—and, well, Clark Gable. Gable, the display said, had joined the army in 1942 after the death of his wife Carole Lombard and served until June of 1944. His visit to Dennison had been shortly after that.

Kim reached for the big machine, positioning her hands one way, then another, and then paused.

"How heavy is this thing?" Debbie asked.

"Very," Kim said. "I'm not sure the best way to pull it out of here."

"I can help with that." They all turned around at the sound of the deep voice, and Janet saw Greg Connor and Sam Watson striding toward them down the hallway. Sam had two thin, round containers of film about the size of an apple pie under his arm. "The door was unlocked. I hope it's okay that we let ourselves in," Greg said.

"Of course," Kim said. "I'm glad you're here."

They stopped just in front of the display case and surveyed the machine. Greg was tall, with broad shoulders and dark hair lightly threaded with gray. Sam Watson was shorter and stockier, with curly hair that must once have been blond, though now it was more gray and faded.

"How about if I grab the bottom and you take the top?" Greg said.

"Let's try it." Sam held out the film cannisters and Janet took them from him. The blue-green metal of the cases was cool under her skin. Janet saw that the top cannister had *#1, September 1944* written on it in black ink, and the second had simply *#2*. There was nothing else on the outside to indicate what was on the film or where it had come from. Then Sam stepped up to the projector, Greg counted to three, and together they hoisted the machine out of the display case and set it on the floor.

"Where would you like it?" Greg asked.

"Let's not try to move it far," Kim said. She pointed to a section of the opposite wall where there was an open white space. "Can you turn it that way, and we can try to see if it will project there?"

"Sure thing." The men lifted the machine once more and positioned it so the lenses were facing the open space. Kim ran to the storage room to get an extension cord—"Make sure it has a surge protector!" Greg insisted—and after she plugged it in, they were all more than surprised when a square of white light appeared on the far wall.

"It actually turned on," Debbie said.

"Now let's see if we can figure out how to get the film into it," Kim said. She pressed a button on the side of the machine and the top part opened. Inside there was a piece that pulled out that had two wheels. It looked kind of like the old film projectors Janet remembered seeing show educational films in the classroom when she was a child.

"That's got to be where the film goes," she said, and Debbie nodded.

"But how do we get it in there?" Kim said.

It took about fifteen minutes of trial and error, but eventually they had one of the rolls of film, the one labeled 1944, loaded into the wheels. They carefully closed the machine.

"Here goes nothing," Kim said, and pressed another button on the side of the machine to start it. When a black-and-white image of a young Eileen Palmer appeared on the screen, they all cheered, and Kim let out a whoop. Eileen wore the dark jacket and hat from her time as the stationmaster at the Dennison Depot. Sam ran over to the light switch and flipped off the overhead lights.

"It's Mom!" Kim said, clapping.

On the screen, Eileen waved, standing in what looked like the door of a train car. The film was grainy by today's standards, but you could make out what was on-screen easily enough.

"Can you tell us how long you've been the stationmaster here at the Dennison Depot?" asked a voice off camera. Janet looked over at Debbie, whose eyes widened. That voice was familiar.

"I took over about a year ago, when the regular stationmaster was called into active military duty," Eileen said. "I was a volunteer here at the canteen before that."

Janet had seen photos of Eileen during her time as stationmaster before, but she'd never seen video footage. It was amazing to see and hear her like this.

"What does a stationmaster do?" the off-screen voice said. Janet felt a shiver of recognition. She knew that voice. At one point, most people in America would have recognized that voice.

On-screen, Eileen talked about how she was responsible for making sure the trains arrived and left as scheduled, how she over-saw safety in the station, and how she looked after the workers, including the porters and the ticket sellers.

"How old are you, Miss Turner?"

"Almost twenty-one."

"It's pretty amazing that someone as young as you are manages this whole station."

"There's a war on. We all have to step up and do our part, and if this is how I can best serve my country, I'm proud to do it," Eileen said. It was incredible to see her so young and full of life, but that wasn't what captivated Janet the most about this interview. Was she crazy? Was her mind playing tricks on her because she wanted to believe it was Clark Gable interviewing Eileen?

Janet wasn't a huge film buff, but she'd gone through a classic movie phase in high school and had fallen in love with famous actors of the times. And Clark Gable was especially easy on the eyes. Could it really be Hollywood's biggest star behind the camera on this film?

The interview with Eileen lasted about ten minutes, and then the film cut to the canteen—now the Whistle Stop Café—where vol-unteers were packing lunches into paper bags by the hundreds. Janet and Debbie both clapped to see their familiar café as it had been back in the forties, when it was the home of the volunteer effort to feed the servicemen who came through Dennison on their way to war.

"Look how great the windows are!" Debbie said.

"And the ceilings! That pressed tin looks so good," Janet added.

"I love the women's outfits," Kim added.

Janet had to admit the outfits in the forties were pretty much the best. The women all wore demure dresses, some with full skirts, as well as dressy shoes and swirled updos. Janet couldn't imagine getting dressed up that nicely for much of anything, let alone a day of making sandwiches.

The man behind the camera started talking to one of the women packing sandwiches. The woman was tall with dark hair, and she wore a no-nonsense button-down dress. The woman looked familiar, though Janet couldn't place her. There was a young girl, maybe a preteen, by her side, with curly dark hair and a wide smile. It took a minute for Janet to realize she knew who the young girl was.

"Is that Gayle?" She turned to Debbie. "Ray Zink's sister?"

Debbie looked closer then said, "Oh my. Yes, I think it is."

Gayle Zink—now Gayle Bailey—lived in Columbus, and was still spry and energetic, even in her nineties. It was surprising to see her here, so young and vibrant. The woman next to her had to be her mother, judging by the similarity in their faces and countenance. On-screen, the mother talked about how every day the women of Dennison came to the depot and volunteered their time to feed and welcome the soldiers who passed through. Janet was riveted. It was so fun seeing a younger version of their friend that for a moment, she forgot why they were viewing the footage at all, until the familiar voice asked the women to show him the doughnut fryer. Janet wondered, once again, whether it truly could be Clark Gable. The voice was so familiar—but did she just *want* it to be him?

The scene in the canteen lasted a few minutes longer, and then the film cut off. The scene shifted, and they saw the inside of an ornate building. It had sumptuous wallpaper and paintings edged with scrolled gilt frames and heavy red drapery. A sparkling chandelier hung from the middle of the room. At first Janet thought it must be a ballroom, but then she saw a counter, backed by mirrors and a case of popcorn, at the far end.

"A theater?" Debbie guessed.

"Wait, is that—"

"That's it!" Sam exclaimed. "That's my theater!"

"Oh my," Janet said. "I don't remember it looking like that, that's for sure." The theater had closed its doors when Janet and Debbie were very young. Janet had a vague memory of having been there once, to see the movie *Annie* with her mother, so that must have been in the early eighties or so. She remembered plush carpets and seats and the smell of popcorn, and the sense that the building was enormous, but that was pretty much all she could call to mind.

"I think a lot of the grandeur had faded by the time you went there," Sam said.

"Look at that concession stand." Debbie shook her head. "That looks like wood."

"That's still there, such as it is," Sam said.

A man walked into the shot and addressed the camera. "My name is Stanley Hersey, and I'm the owner of Sunshine Cinemas."

"Mr. Hersey, can you tell us what it's been like to own a theater since the war started?" the familiar voice asked.

"Well, it's been tough, of course," Stanley said. "On the one hand, Americans need distraction, and there are plenty of good films being produced. On the other hand, so many men are overseas fighting that it's hard to sell enough tickets sometimes. Of course, all soldiers returning from war get a free movie ticket here at Sunshine Cinemas, yourself included." He ducked his head at the camera.

"Why thank you very much. I will take you up on that offer."

"It would be an honor, Mr. Gable."

A man stepped into the shot from off-screen and reached out and shook the theater owner's hand, and everyone in the room gasped.

There he was. He was instantly recognizable. There was no mistaking that smile, that signature mustache. Standing in the lobby of the old theater was Hollywood legend Clark Gable.

Which meant that this was very likely part of the film project he had shot in Dennison in 1944. The film reels that had been reported stolen.

So how had they ended up buried in the wall of the old theater?

A NOTE FROM the EDITORS

We hope you enjoyed another exciting volume in the Whistle Stop Café Mysteries series, published by Guideposts. For over seventy-five years, Guideposts, a nonprofit organization, has been driven by a vision of a world filled with hope. We aspire to be the voice of a trusted friend, a friend who makes you feel more hopeful and connected.

By making a purchase from Guideposts, you join our community in touching millions of lives, inspiring them to believe that all things are possible through faith, hope, and prayer. Your continued support allows us to provide uplifting resources to those in need. Whether through our communities, websites, apps, or publications, we inspire our audiences, bring them together, and comfort, uplift, entertain, and guide them. Visit us at guideposts.org to learn more.

We would love to hear from you. Write us at Guideposts, P.O. Box 5815, Harlan, Iowa 51593 or call us at (800) 932-2145. Did you love *Now You're in My Arms*? Leave a review for this product on guideposts.org/shop. Your feedback helps others in our community find relevant products.

Find inspiration, find faith, find Guideposts.

Shop our best sellers and favorites at

guideposts.org/shop

Or scan the QR code to go directly to our Shop

While you are waiting for the next fascinating story in the Whistle Stop Café Mysteries, check out some other Guideposts mystery series!

SECRETS FROM GRANDMA'S ATTIC

Life is recorded not only in decades or years, but in events and memories that form the fabric of our being. Follow Tracy Doyle, Amy Allen, and Robin Davisson, the granddaughters of the recently deceased centenarian, Pearl Allen, as they explore the treasures found in the attic of Grandma Pearl's Victorian home, nestled near the banks of the Mississippi in Canton, Missouri. Not only do Pearl's descendants uncover a long-buried mystery at every attic exploration, they also discover their grandmother's legacy of deep, abiding faith, which has shaped and guided their family through the years. These uncovered Secrets from Grandma's Attic reveal stories of faith, redemption, and second chances that capture your heart long after you turn the last page.

History Lost and Found
The Art of Deception
Testament to a Patriot
Buttoned Up

Pearl of Great Price

Hidden Riches

Movers and Shakers

The Eye of the Cat

Refined by Fire

The Prince and the Popper

Something Shady

Duel Threat

A Royal Tea

The Heart of a Hero

Fractured Beauty

A Shadowy Past

In Its Time

Nothing Gold Can Stay

The Cameo Clue

Veiled Intentions

Turn Back the Dial

A Marathon of Kindness

A Thief in the Night

Coming Home

SAVANNAH SECRETS

Welcome to Savannah, Georgia, a picture-perfect Southern city known for its manicured parks, moss-covered oaks, and antebellum architecture. Walk down one of the cobblestone streets, and you'll come upon Magnolia Investigations. It is here where two friends have joined forces to unravel some of Savannah's deepest secrets. Tag along as clues are exposed, red herrings discarded, and thrilling surprises revealed. Find inspiration in the special bond between Meredith Bellefontaine and Julia Foley. Cheer the friends on as they listen to their hearts and rely on their faith to solve each new case that comes their way.

The Hidden Gate
A Fallen Petal
Double Trouble
Whispering Bells
Where Time Stood Still
The Weight of Years
Willful Transgressions
Season's Meetings
Southern Fried Secrets
The Greatest of These
Patterns of Deception

The Waving Girl
Beneath a Dragon Moon
Garden Variety Crimes
Meant for Good
A Bone to Pick
Honeybees & Legacies
True Grits
Sapphire Secret
Jingle Bell Heist
Buried Secrets
A Puzzle of Pearls
Facing the Facts
Resurrecting Trouble
Forever and a Day

MYSTERIES *of* MARTHA'S VINEYARD

Priscilla Latham Grant has inherited a lighthouse! So with not much more than a strong will and a sore heart, the recent widow says goodbye to her lifelong Kansas home and heads to the quaint and historic island of Martha's Vineyard, Massachusetts. There, she comes face-to-face with adventures, which include her trusty canine friend, Jake, three delightful cousins she didn't know she had, and Gerald O'Bannon, a handsome Coast Guard captain—plus head-scratching mysteries that crop up with surprising regularity.

A Light in the Darkness
Like a Fish Out of Water
Adrift
Maiden of the Mist
Making Waves
Don't Rock the Boat
A Port in the Storm
Thicker Than Water
Swept Away
Bridge Over Troubled Waters
Smoke on the Water
Shifting Sands
Shark Bait
Seascape in Shadows

Storm Tide

Water Flows Uphill

Catch of the Day

Beyond the Sea

Wider Than an Ocean

Sheeps Passing in the Night

Sail Away Home

Waves of Doubt

Lifeline

Flotsam & Jetsam

Just Over the Horizon

Find more inspiring stories in these best-loved Guideposts fiction series!

Mysteries of Lancaster County

Follow the Classen sisters as they unravel clues and uncover hidden secrets in Mysteries of Lancaster County. As you get to know these women and their friends, you'll see how God brings each of them together for a fresh start in life.

Secrets of Wayfarers Inn

Retired schoolteachers find themselves owners of an old warehouse-turned-inn that is filled with hidden passages, buried secrets, and stunning surprises that will set them on a course to puzzling mysteries from the Underground Railroad.

Tearoom Mysteries Series

Mix one stately Victorian home, a charming lakeside town in Maine, and two adventurous cousins with a passion for tea and hospitality. Add a large scoop of intriguing mystery, and sprinkle generously with faith, family, and friends, and you have the recipe for *Tearoom Mysteries*.

Ordinary Women of the Bible

Richly imagined stories—based on facts from the Bible—have all the plot twists and suspense of a great mystery, while bringing you fascinating insights on what it was like to be a woman living in the ancient world.

To learn more about these books, visit Guideposts.org/Shop